SAFE AND SOUND

A RENTER-FRIENDLY GUIDE TO HOME REPAIR

MERCURY STARDUST

SAFE AND SOUND

A RENTER-FRIENDLY GUIDE TO HOME REPAIR

DK

Publisher Mike Sanders
Senior Editor Molly Ahuja
Art Director William Thomas
Assistant Art Director Becky Batchelor
Cover and Lifestyle Illustrations Grier Hunt
Technical Illustrations May van Millingen
Photography Hillary Schave Azena Photography
Proofreader Claire Safran
Indexer Beverlee Day

First American Edition, 2023
Published in the United States by DK Publishing
6081 E 82nd St, Suite 400, Indianapolis, IN 46250

The authorized representative in the EEA is Dorling Kindersley
Verlag GmbH. Arnulfstr. 124, 80636 Munich, Germany

A catalog record for this book
is available from the Library of Congress.
ISBN 978-0-7440-7907-4

DK books are available at special discounts when purchased
in bulk for sales promotions, premiums, fund-raising, or
educational use. For details, contact SpecialSales@dk.com

Printed and bound in Italy

For the curious
www.dk.com

CONTENTS

HEY THERE, HI!

Dear Reader,

Hey there, hi! My name is Mercury Stardust, also known as the Trans Handy Ma'am. As my name would suggest, I am a very proud Transwoman and also a virtual home maintenance technician and certified repair expert. I have been in this field for over 16 years, working with renters, landlords, homeowners, and businesses in tropical Madison, Wisconsin. Many of those years I was perceived as a man, all the while hiding who I was. When I transitioned from being "one of the guys" to being a woman, I was treated entirely differently by my peers and employers. the contrast hit me like a bolt of lighting, but ultimately, it became my motivational drive and gave me the best tool I have in my tool bag: compassion. I realize that there is a special kind of corniness that comes with that last notion, but as the kids would say, that's very "on brand" for me. There is a fundamental thread that runs throughout everything I do:

"There is no such thing as common sense."

We all come from different backgrounds with different lived experiences, which can lead to amazing knowledge in some aspects of one's life though maybe not in others. **But there is a universal truth: We all panic when the toilet overflows.** We reach for anything nearby to soak up the dirty water; we scream for help from whoever will be in earshot. Those moments are filled with desperation and often anger that we should've known better. I'm not here to berate you for not knowing how to turn off the water to your toilet. I am here to teach you how to do it. You should never be ashamed for not knowing something you were never taught.

If we all have these same overwhelming feelings around home emergencies, then why does most DIY content only focus on homeowners and not on renters? Renters (a whopping 36% of Americans) should have the same feeling of empowerment. They have toilets that overflow, sinks that clog, doors that jam, mold growing in the bathroom, and so many other things that may need fixing. They are told to reach out to landlords when they need something repaired but are too often ignored or find themselves waiting endlessly when the work is delayed. While existing home-repair books may explain some of the skills *homeowners* need in these desperate situations, they rarely take into account how a tenant's approach can differ from that of a homeowner. For instance, a renter may not know or be able to determine the material of their pipes when dealing with a plumbing issue, or they may not have the authority to simply replace outdated appliances or parts. There are very few, if any, how-to books aimed at a renter's experiences and needs, and that's where this book comes in.

In addition to the fundamentals of home repair, this book will provide important information regarding choosing an apartment that works best for one's individual needs, and the pitfalls to avoid when it comes to placing work orders, keeping your deposit, and irascible or absent landlords. You will also be given essential and tailored advice on how to grow a collection of tools—one focused on building a foundation of core tools that everyone should have in their home. In the largest section of the book, I'll teach you step-by-step home repairs covering the most common issues I've seen during my career. We'll finish with important information on safety and security, moving out of your home, and information regarding tenant rights and the resources you can reach out to if those laws are being violated. Throughout the text, you will find the gentle and affirming words of encouragement that I'm most known for e.g., "If you don't own, it doesn't mean your space is less of a home!" or "You are worth the time it takes to learn a new skill!" This book is also highly visual, with detailed illustrations, QR codes with links to videos, and personal videos recorded by me to give you the pep talk you might need to keep going with your projects. These images and videos are used throughout to help you feel confident when beginning each DIY project.

Thank you for taking the time to read this. Regardless of if you've purchased this book, been given it as a gift, are giving it as a gift, or are just browsing through it at the bookstore, I hope you leave this introduction with a little more perspective, and little more compassion in your own bag of tricks. I'll leave you with the same goodbye I give at the end of every video, "Have a good day, take care and, buh-bye!"

Mercury Stardust
"The Trans Handy Ma'am"
Virtual Maintenance Technician

PART 1

★

THE
BASICS

1

APARTMENT HUNTING

HOME SWEET HOME

The process of looking for a home, especially a rental, can be a terrifying one. Trust me, I feel your pain. On top of my years of experience working in apartments as a maintenance technician, I am a lifelong renter who has moved seven times within the past six years. I know exactly how daunting this task can be, particularly for those taking it on by themselves or for the first time. The goal of this chapter is to help guide you through the process of finding a place to call home. There are so many red flags to look for in a potential apartment, but being a more informed tenant will help protect you from bad landlords and bad situations.

To start, you first have to find a place you can afford in a neighborhood that makes sense for your lifestyle. But is it safe? Will you be able to park or get to public transportation? What about your bike—is there a secure place to lock it up? Maybe you've found the perfect spot that fits all your needs but the landlord requires you earn four times the rent or the place gets scooped up before you have a chance to tour it!

BIG FEELINGS, LITTLE FEELINGS

"It might seem obvious to some, but I believe it's important to take a moment to acknowledge that finding a new home is difficult."

It might seem obvious to some, but I believe it's important to take a moment to acknowledge that finding a new home is difficult. Not only does it take time and effort to search for the right rental, pack your belongings, and transport them somewhere new, but one's home is an incredibly personal space. Moving is hard. Change is hard. Especially if you're neurodivergent or have survived trauma.

This process is even more difficult for members of marginalized communities. The United States has a long history of baking racism and other forms of discrimination into law and the resulting institutional racism is alive and well in the housing industry. Redlining, exclusionary zoning, minimum lot sizes, and other racist practices have created a housing market that forces nonwhite people into rentals, but a 2021 study by the National Bureau of Economic Research noted that these same people are shown fewer apartments and receive fewer replies to inquiries than their white peers.

For much of my professional career, I worked in neighborhoods with affordable housing that were considered "unsafe" by wealthier residents of Madison, Wisconsin. More than 80% of the tenants I worked with were nonwhite, recent immigrants, refugees, trans people, or in need of assisted living. This wasn't proportionate to the city I inhabited, where 72.9% of the population is white and 88.1% were born in the United States. Discrimination is a real, invasive issue in the rental market. Don't let anyone gaslight you into believing anything else.

We can't continue our conversation about renting without acknowledging this reality. I'm a white person and I want to be honest about the fact that my privilege has informed my understanding of this process. However, as a trans woman, I've experienced the emotional weight of trying to find a home in a system that wasn't built for you. When you begin looking for an apartment and as you work through the steps of moving in, I encourage you to check in with yourself. Take breaks when you can, reach out to your support systems, and remember that it's okay if you're feeling overwhelmed or defeated. We all know that apartment hunting isn't fun, but the emotional component is rarely discussed. I want you to feel safe in your home and your mental health is a vital part of establishing that sense of security.

"I encourage you to check in with yourself. Take breaks when you can, reach out to your support systems, and remember that it's okay if you're feeling overwhelmed or defeated."

FIGURING OUT FINANCING

First things first, we have to talk about finances. You'll hear advice that suggests you should only be spending 30% of your monthly income on your home. I don't want to focus on that number. Feeling safe in your home should be your number one priority. If that means you have to spend more than 30% of your monthly income on rent, that's okay. Too frequently, conversations about finances are filled with shame—shame that you're not making enough money and shame for not being good at budgeting. I'm here to tell you that those negative comments are wrong. Do what you need to do to keep yourself and your family safe—and don't let others shame you into housing that puts you in a vulnerable situation.

Not only are these unhelpful budgeting "tips" based on outdated numbers, but they rarely take into account issues of accessibility. Housing that's accessible to renters with limited mobility is frequently far more expensive, as are buildings close to public transportation or well-maintained sidewalks. Your needs will inform how you build your budget and that result is going to look different for everyone.

Of course, I'm not suggesting you spend 100% of your income on your apartment. Be mindful of how much money you can afford monthly and

try to find the best rental you can in that range. Remember that housing in major cities is often far more expensive and that your budget might look very different if you're moving somewhere new. For example, in New York City, you might need to spend half your income on rent, but you don't necessarily need a car, eliminating gas, insurance, and other costs associated with a vehicle. Whereas in rural Maine, you might be able to find much cheaper rent, but you'll need a reliable car that's safe in the snow. There are many factors that can come into play here: Cities with extreme weather might result in higher heating or electrical bills; areas with food apartheids could require higher gas or grocery bills; bigger cities can provide easier access to free or sliding-scale health care. As you think about your price range, rank your financial needs and consider how the resources available in your area can inform your housing budget.

I'm not going to give you a hard number or percentage of what you "should" be spending because this isn't a one-size-fits-all issue. You do your best to find a price range that works for your situation and I'll do my best to make sure you have the knowledge you need to keep you safe and comfortable in your home.

SAFE AS A BUG
IN A RUG

Let's get into the meat and potatoes of this chapter. How many entry points does your potential home have? I know this might not be the most fun topic of conversation, but it's important to know how many points of access exist in the apartment. This number can vary widely depending on what level the unit is on or the type of building it's in.

Let's start by talking about apartments that are on the first floor. How many doors come from the outside into your apartment? Do the windows slide or do they crank open? Typically, it's easier and more possible for someone to break into your apartment through a window with a crank. Does your main door open directly to the outside or does it go through a lobby? Lobbies provide an extra layer of protection. Are other access points to your home visible to your neighbors or are they down a dark alley? These are all little aspects to think about when you're living on the ground level.

What about pets? Personally, I have two amazing cats, Apollo and Nitro. We live in a ground-floor apartment and the cats definitely appreciate the little bunnies and squirrels they get to see frolicking around outside. While there's a safety risk living on the first floor, I considered the fact that I'm nestled into a little community of apartment buildings. Every entry point into my home is well lit and visible by someone else's apartment. There are cameras all around my building and our property management company hired security to do nightly patrols of the parking lot and surrounding area.

That said, ground-floor apartments can have their advantages. I'd much rather move my furniture into a first-floor apartment than one on the fifth floor. Not only does the ground floor have a clear advantage when moving, but you should also consider your everyday activities. Do you go grocery shopping every day or once a week? It's far easier to carry large loads and make multiple trips to a first-floor space, especially if you have small children in tow. It's all about weighing your priorities and deciding what's most important to you.

If you're reading this as someone who's living in a second-floor apartment with a balcony and you're giggling to yourself, thinking, "Ha! I'd never live on the first floor," I have a little story for you. Several years back, I was working at a property where several of the buildings had catwalks linking one apartment to another. Directly below the catwalk was the main sidewalk leading into the building. From the sidewalk to the bottom of the catwalk was about 10 feet, which I thought was sufficient to keep people safe. To get into people's apartments, one had to go through the locked front door and then up the staircase. Well, one night as I was leaving the property, I saw a young man run up from a sidewalk, jump, grab the bottom of the catwalk, and pull himself up. I was flabbergasted. I ran up to the railing to check and inspect it, and it was obvious the railing was now extremely loose. That would indicate that this wasn't a one-time occurrence but was happening on a regular basis. I installed a flare guard so you couldn't just grab the railing with your hands. I took away the open-faced railing and put in an enclosed railing. After weeks and weeks of work, I was yet again heading home when I saw another young man quickly climb a nearby tree and leap onto the catwalk. Shortly thereafter, I left the company and never got to hear the end of the saga, but even if they cut down that tree, I feel like those young boys were determined to get home in the most inefficient way possible.

All this is to say that being on the second floor doesn't necessarily mean you're safe from intruders. Fortunately, the boys climbing the railings in this instance were residents, but their actions made me aware of a major potential security risk. If there's a catwalk or balcony that leads to a door going into your apartment, please check how high up it is. Can someone access that with a ladder, from a nearby tree, or simply by jumping?

Lastly, when you think about security, it's important to remember that it's not just about keeping people out. The higher up in an apartment building you live, the harder it might be for you to leave in the event of a fire or another emergency. Can everyone in your household run down the stairs if necessary? Does the apartment have well-maintained fire escapes or can you use a collapsible window ladder?

I know this can feel like a lot of information to take in all at once. It's okay if feelings of fear or anxiety are coming up as you read this, but try not to panic just yet. None of these safety concerns have to be deal-breakers. Safety isn't that black and white, and in fact, in Chapter 13, I'll go over ways to make your home more secure.

Having a few safety concerns can sometimes be the price of admission in the rental market and my words are meant as a guide. You get to decide what safety features are most important to you.

VIEWING YOUR HOPEFUL HOME

SEE THE SPACE

When you're looking for a new home, you'll often have the opportunity to tour an apartment. Make sure you can look at the specific unit you'd be living in. If you're moving across the country and not available to be there in person, ask if you could do a virtual tour in the apartment unit that you'll be renting.

You might already know to check the water pressure and look inside the fridge, but it's also important to see the actual space you'll be living in so you can look for wear and tear in the home. When I tour an apartment, I want to see how dinged up the walls are and how worn the carpeting is. I want to see all the things that could potentially cause issues once I'm living there. Note whether the apartment complex allows you to view the apartment while the current tenants are living there because this will indicate if you'll have to deal with viewings when it comes time for you to move out. It's also best to try to tour the apartment during typically busier times, such as when people are getting ready for work or when they get home in the evenings because this will give you a chance to see what the noise levels are like with your neighbors and the location.

"Having a few safety concerns can sometimes be the price of admission in the rental market and my words are meant as a guide."

Over the years, I've heard many scams where property managers offer tours of a demo apartment rather than the actual unit for rent. These apartments are often freshly furnished and well taken care of because they're the company's chance to put their best foot forward. However, because no one is living in these spaces, no natural wear and tear can occur. It's important to gauge how quickly the materials in your potential apartment are aging because it gives you insights into their quality. A great example of this is with carpeted floors. If you're touring an apartment and you notice the carpet is worn out, ask how long ago it was installed. This could indicate if the company is using cheap, easily damaged materials. Many apartment complexes will be quick to place blame on the tenant, but I've seen time and time again that the materials used in an apartment are often the actual culprit.

It's also important to remember that when you're viewing the apartment for the first time, you won't have much more than 15 or 20 minutes in the space. Having a few questions prepared before the meeting can go a long way toward helping you find the right home. In addition to the questions I've already gone over, I like to ask how long a typical tenant stays in this apartment. Alternatively, you could ask how many tenants have stayed in the apartment complex for more than five years. Learning how long past renters have chosen to stay in your potential apartment can indicate what it might be like living there.

Another essential question for your property manager is how many people have access to your apartment. Thanks to universal keys, some units might be accessible to 10–30 people. This could include the entire team of maintenance technicians, including part-timers or emergency techs, property managers for the entire company, and even owners of the building, who you wouldn't normally come in contact with. While this isn't necessarily something you can change, it can be important information in helping you make your decision.

MEET THE TECH

Asking if you can meet with a maintenance technician is also very informative. Because of their busy schedule, you might not be able to have the opportunity to meet them ahead of time, but they can offer helpful information if you have the chance.

When I was a maintenance technician, I rarely missed the opportunity to meet a new tenant. I understood the importance of developing a relationship with people who'd be relying on me in a moment of need. If you do get the opportunity to meet, I'd ask how often they've worked on the specific unit you might be renting. If they're there every three to six weeks, something larger might be going on and this could be a red flag. It could indicate there's a problem they can't solve or they aren't solving a problem properly. Meeting the maintenance technician prior to moving can also allow you to gauge their expertise. Not all handypersons are created equally and some states don't even require basic certifications in important areas like electrical and plumbing.

Remember that it's okay if asking any of these questions intimidates you. Not only can finding a home be stressful, but meeting new people or being in a new environment can also trigger feelings of anxiety. If the idea of meeting with a technician on top of all that is more than you can handle, I want you to know those feelings are very real and valid. You can always send a follow-up email later asking if they'd be open to answering your questions.

CHECK OUT THE AMENITIES

While you're in an apartment, be sure to check all the appliances and note their location in the building. Do you have a bathroom attached to your bedroom or is it shared? Do you have a washer and dryer in your unit or is it elsewhere in the building? Will you have a microwave, oven, refrigerator, dishwasher, or none of the above? Having an idea of what you want prior to going will help you narrow down your search.

I want to take a moment to note that it's perfectly normal not to have any of these things in your home. Many of the appliances I've listed here are a luxury. Their presence in an apartment will often up the price of rent and it's okay if they're out of your budget.

It's important to check out any extra spaces that might be included in your rent. If they offer a storage unit, make sure you ask to see it. This is often an indication of how they treat the rest of the building. If the storage units are large closets and have very secure locks, this could indicate a place you can rely on. If the storage unit is just chicken wire and particleboard, take that into consideration. Don't forget to ask if they're having any issues with theft because they're legally required to tell you the truth.

If the apartment offers parking, be sure to check out the area where your space would be. Is it in a covered garage? In an adjacent lot? How far of a walk is it to your front door? If you're visiting during the day, be sure to note whether streetlights cover the area or if they've installed motion-activated lights. If none of these features exist, you might ask the property manager whether their company offers security in the area.

READING THE LEASE

If all goes well and you're ready to take the next step with the apartment, be sure to read the lease carefully. This contract can be very intimidating if you aren't familiar with legal language and it's important not to beat yourself up if you don't understand everything right away. It's okay to ask for clarifications from the property manager or reach out to a friend or family member you trust. Your best tool when reading the lease will be knowing your local laws and regulations. Never sign a lease that violates the law. Check out Chapter 15 to see if there's a nearby organization that can help explain the local laws in clear, accessible language.

Between my years renting and working with property managers, I've seen some very bad leases, so here are some of the red flags I look for when I'm entering into a new agreement:

- Language that allows the landlord to change the terms after the lease has been signed.
- Expensive late rent fees.
- Waivers or any language that releases the property manager from being responsible for pre-existing issues (mold being a common example).
- Language that limits the number of guests you can have in your home or how long they can stay.
- Vague language about how long the landlord has to get your deposit back to you. They should offer a clear timeline and ideally a schedule of charges for the return of your security deposit.
- A lack of information about why and how you could be evicted.

Some of these might feel self-explanatory, but I want to take a moment to zoom in on the issue of liability. At one of my more recent jobs was a tenant who had filed a request to fix her flooding basement. It had been quite some time since the request was filed and the woman who lived in the apartment had recently lost her 17-year-old son and was having a hard time. She was understandably devastated and now her basement was flooding on top of everything else. I saw her one day and she let me know how upset and angry she was that the issue hadn't been resolved. Seeing the pain in her eyes, I agreed to come take a look that evening after my shift had ended. When I went down into the basement, it was clear the situation was stemming from a much larger issue and that I'd need to talk to the property owners about the substantial repair. The next day, I brought up the issue with my supervisor and they immediately brushed it off. "It was in the lease that the basement floods, so we don't have to do anything about it," they said. I was shocked and quite upset by their lack of empathy for this woman, but it taught me an important lesson.

I share this story to illustrate that even if something doesn't seem like a big deal right now, it might become one down the line. There are many things in life we can't predict, but waivers of liability are a good indication that something has happened in the past and will probably happen again in the future. If you're on the fence about an apartment with a liability waiver, make sure you understand the potential issues that could stem from whatever they're informing you about. You know yourself best and you know what you can handle, so make sure you're fully informed about what you're taking on before you make a final decision.

While there can obviously be some major red flags in leases, there's also a lot of information that's simply helpful to know. These points can help you understand how you'll interact with the people working in the building:

- A set schedule or time frame for how long the management company has to complete a repair.
- A clearly written policy about how and when property managers or maintenance technicians are allowed to enter your apartment. Ideally, you want to have a hard copy on hand or the company should be able to provide one for you on request.

That might feel like a lot of language to look out for and it's okay if you're feeling overwhelmed. Remember that you should be able to look over the lease on your own before signing, allowing you time and space to read through the contract carefully and look up any terms you don't totally understand. The good news is that while there are a lot of potential red flags in a lease, you also have the opportunity to add terms that benefit you during this process. Some examples of terms I've seen included:

- Adding an extra parking spot or storage unit if needed.
- Requiring that the company replace carpeting seven years after the initial installation.
- Rules about how frequently or what percentage rent can be raised.
- A lower rent if you won't be using a parking space or storage unit that's included in the rate.

I won't lie to you: Negotiating a lease can be a scary process, but it can also be a helpful tool in predicting how your property management company will treat you if issues arise down the line. If you're feeling really anxious, you can always ask a friend to come with you for support or request changes to the lease via email. Negotiating the lease through email can give you more time to process their responses, and as an added plus, it will ensure that any promises the landlord makes are in writing.

Emotional Reset

Before I move on to the next chapter about the move-in process, let's take a moment to reflect. I've gone over a ton of information already and feeling overloaded is a completely valid reaction to learning about the rental process. Your home is an incredibly personal place and it's natural for big feelings to come up as you think about or begin the process of moving. It's okay to take a break or revisit portions of this book when you need to.

Let's also remember how I started this chapter: with the idea that you deserve a safe, comfortable space to live regardless of your circumstances. If you choose to live somewhere with one of the "red flags" I've mentioned in this chapter, that doesn't mean you've done anything wrong. Please never blame or gaslight yourself if your best option is less than ideal. You deserve safety and respect in your home. Always. Things might not be perfect the day you move in, but that doesn't mean they have to stay that way—and this book is here to help.

2

MOVING IN AND CREATING A HOME

THE CHECKITY CHECKLIST

When you first move into your apartment, you're going to get a checklist that's going to have a list of different things in the home for you to look at and determine the state of. I can't advise enough to always write out thoroughly everything on the checklist. Make sure every appliance works, every door is checked, every piece of trim if reviewed, and every nook and cranny of the walls is looked at. Write down every single thing.

"Make sure every appliance works, every door is checked, every piece of trim if reviewed, and every nook and cranny of the walls is looked at."

And for your posterity, make sure you take photos of every single thing you see. Every room, every wall, every door, every appliance, everything. Document it and put it into Google Drive or on a USB drive, and make sure you have it when you move out. No matter how long you're there, you need to make sure you protect yourself from other people's decisions.

- Look for signs of pests—for example, mouse droppings that might look like little seeds or dark grains of rice that are in the cabinets or on the floor. Check to see if there are other signs of pests, like roaches, bugs, or other rodents, that might be roaming in your apartment.
- Run every single drain in your home to see if it drains properly or if there's a clog. Make sure you put in a notice right away and write on that list if it never gets taken care of.
- Check every door to see if it latches properly, and if it doesn't, write that on the list and put in a maintenance request.
- If there are scrapes, holes, etc., in the wall that aren't properly repaired, put that on the list too. You don't want to be accused of trying to do a poor patch when you're moving out when the patch was already there when you moved in.
- Take a look at the carpet at the back of closets. Is the carpet pulled up? Is it damaged? Really make sure the carpet everywhere, including the back of any closet, is sealed well and ready to go.
- Check every light fixture in the home, every toilet, every faucet, every tub you might have, including the showerhead.
- Check the water shut-off valves in the kitchen, bathrooms, and at the toilets to make sure they turn on and off easily. They should turn by hand and not need any tools or additional leverage.
- See how the water pressure is in the shower.

- Check all the cabinets in the kitchen to make sure they open properly.
- Look for any floor damage throughout the apartment.
- Don't forget to document the storage unit if you have one. If you have a garage, storage unit, or anything else that's attached to your lease, also check those; if there isn't a section for those on the checklist, you can always add it.

And if you run out of room on the sheet you were given, you can always attach a sheet on the back of it and put as many pieces of paper as you want. You're allowed to write down every single flaw you want and that's going to protect you later on. When in doubt, document, document, document. I also recommend scanning the document or taking photos of it and saving the whole document prior to turning it in. To be extra safe, after turning the physical copy in, you can also send it as an attachment in an email to the landlord or property manager.

I can't stress enough the importance of this checklist and the thoroughness of it! It can help you get your deposit back when you can prove that damages or the state of the apartment was like that when you moved in.

CONSTRUCTION-GRADE MATERIALS

In most apartments, you'll find what's called "construction-grade materials." If you've never heard the term "construction grade," it refers to the grade of material that you have in your home. This often refers to windows, faucets, cabinets, doors, etc. There are four different grades you want to be aware of:

- Builder
- Quality
- Custom
- Ultra-custom

We're going to leave custom and ultra-custom off this list and talk about "builder grade" and "quality grade" because these are the ones you're most likely to encounter in your apartment search.

Builder grade is the most common in apartments. Apartment companies, property management companies, and landlords tend to buy things in bulk. When they buy in bulk, they buy a lot of something for a reduced price from a warehouse, hardware store, or larger supply company. And when they do this, they typically buy builder grade. This is where you get your flush-mounted lights, your lower-end faucets, your hollow-core doors, etc.

Because this is builder grade, it's not great long term and it typically isn't super durable. Builder grade will also include inexpensive wood products, such as particleboard or cheaper plywood. And the metal often used will be nickel or a similar material that can be damaged and dented fairly quickly. Builder grade is also sometimes called "contractor grade." Both of those refer to the construction of the building or the renovation of the space when it was being done.

Quality grade is what we're looking for because it will be more durable. But there's a pervasive ideology that landlords and property management companies have where they think, "Why put quality-grade equipment into homes when you know the tenant or renters are going to damage it." You hear this constantly when it comes to towel racks, for example.

Instead of putting in a strong quality-grade piece of equipment, they put in aluminum racks. Those aluminum racks sometimes fall apart and can cause damage to a wall. And the reason why they use aluminum over a solid piece of metal is because they believe renters are just going to rip out the quality-grade equipment or break it, instead of the builder-grade material simply breaking over time on its own.

These choices lead to bigger issues. I was in people's homes much more often as a maintenance technician constantly repairing and fixing low-grade equipment that's not holding up over time. Renters are often people who are viewed as lesser just because they're renters, and because it's not their property, rental companies think they're overly abusive to the equipment and materials in their home.

The reality is this idea comes from an antagonistic point of view of a landlord and property management. I've been a renter for all my adult life and I've never purposely tried to damage anything. Lived-in homes will simply have a lived-in experience. But if you have lower-grade equipment, such as builder grade, then you're going to have larger problems. And I always err on the side of caution and don't recommend them.

Here's what you want to look for when touring a new home:

- You can typically figure out if a metal is lower grade if it's not magnetic. If you've got a magnet with you and put it on something and it's not holding it, chances are it's aluminum or nickel.

- Particleboard is fairly easy to spot. If you see particleboard in various parts of the home, it's probably being covered up with some type of sticky sealant. And you can spot that by seeing how much of a flash or sheen it has or how the seams just appear to be held together with glue. Solid wood, solid countertops, and a solid door are going to be better for you.

- If you knock on a solid-core door, it's going to sound hollow. If you knock on the door and it sounds like it's solid wood, you're not dealing with builder grade—you're dealing with quality-grade equipment.

Remember, it's okay if your home has builder-grade equipment. Take care of it as best as you can, but know that if it wears out or breaks quickly, it's not your fault. Don't let your landlord place blame or guilt on you—and you can always request they replace it with a higher-quality item that won't break so easily.

CREATING A HOME

I'm not much of an interior designer. I can't tell you exactly how to make sure your home is laid out to be hip and popular with the masses—that's not my expertise! What **is** my expertise is making sure you make your house or apartment feel like a home.

There are going to be standards that tell you don't match this with that, don't put this there, do this with your windows, and do this with your doors—and all this might make you feel like somebody else out there is the expert in making your space feel like your home. The reality is no one else knows how to create your home quite like you.

Your home is unique to you and what matters most is: Does it function in a way that makes you feel safe? Does it look a way that makes you feel loved? Does it remind you of things that make you feel good?

"Your home is unique to you and what matters most is: Does it function in a way that makes you feel safe? Does it look a way that makes you feel loved? Does it remind you of things that make you feel good?"

To me, all those things outweigh the interior design rules you might have been told. The simple truth is this: If you're somebody who has clutter in their home (like me) and you're sometimes a mess, this doesn't mean your home is less beautiful. There's this whole notion that a home has to be gorgeous to everybody, but the truth is your home only has to make sense to you and everyone who lives in it.

I think it's best to make sure your home is something you can move freely through—that there's not too much in your way so you don't feel claustrophobic. It's best to make sure of a few things when it comes to safety:

- Don't block vents, lighting, or entryways.
- Make sure your objects and furniture is at least 3–4 feet (92–122cm) away from any heat source, like a radiator.
- Know all your emergency exits.
- Identify where smoke and carbon monoxide detectors are.
- If your bed or furniture has to be next to a large window, make sure to weatherize properly to avoid cold drafts in the winter.

All those things are important to creating a home and living your life as comfortably as possible.

It's also important when you're designing the layout of your spaces to not forget about the tools! Where are your tools going to go? You can tuck them away in the back of a closet or the back of a cabinet, but they should have their own home. They deserve a home just as much as you do because your tools will take care of you in a time of need. Make sure you have a toolbox and a dedicated tool space that can grow and expand as you learn more. If you take care of your tools, your tools will take care of you for a long time—it's a give-and-take that's important and often overlooked.

There are also some undeniable facts about the colors we choose to bring into our homes that are good to keep in mind. A light-colored paint on your walls is going to brighten up a room and expand it. It's going to help make it look larger than it is. But being colorful can also bring feelings of joy and serenity when you paint a room. As long as you have that permission from the landlord and you're aware of any restrictions, there's absolutely nothing wrong with that!

People are often afraid to customize their rental home, but it just takes another coat of paint to return it back to its original state when you moved in.

One thing I also like to recommend is that when you're laying out the couches or any other large furniture that you're planning out your space before you move everything in, especially if you live in a smaller home. Even grabbing a piece of paper to draw exactly how the room will be laid out, such as where you're going to put your big objects, like your TV, bed, couch, dining room table, etc., can help you visualize where everything will go.

While you decide where all the big things are going to go, also make sure you include where the vents are located, where the windows are located, and the exit points for safety—all those things are going to make a big difference. When you're living in tight spaces, it can often be important to get it right the first time and not have to continuously move everything around. It can be hard to do, and every time you move something big, the chances of damaging the area around it increases.

Homes aren't one-size-fits-all, and however the space is going to be laid out, it should work best for you. If you're an artist, you should have a space you can create art in. If you're someone who loves to build things, there should be a space where you can build. If you're someone who loves games and puzzles, make the space that. There are so many products, ideas, Pinterest boards, etc. They can show you how to live in spaces that are cramped and still have them fit your lifestyle.

And in the rest of this book, you'll learn how to customize your space safely and easily as well as return it to its original state to get your deposit back. So hang those curtains and pictures, paint those walls, and feel great in your home!

SETTING YOURSELF UP FOR SUCCESS

In an ideal world, you'd never have to worry about your landlord, property manager, or maintenance technician ever taking advantage of you. In an ideal world, all these people would have your back, support you, and absolutely never want anything bad to happen to you.

But unfortunately, that's not the world we live in. We live in a reality that's sometimes a little bit stressful and scary. I'm going to help you out the best I can with the information I have in this book to set you up for success—whether it's your first rental home or your 15th.

DOCUMENTATION

One of the things I want you to do when you're moving into a new home is to take pictures and video. This is one of the most important things you could ever do. Make sure every single thing is accounted for with a visual aid, labeled, and put into a digital folder to keep in case of a negligent landlord or when you attempt to get your security deposit back.

It's important to know exactly how the space was before you moved in, so document any damage that occurs during the time you're there. Get comfortable with the idea of documenting everything to best communicate what's happening to your landlord but also potentially a judge. It's always scary to talk about legal things when discussing homes, but as a renter, you need to know the legal ins and outs just as much as homeowners need to understand mortgages. Understanding the legality of everything you're partaking in is vital.

You need to really document what you're seeing. You have the advantage of having so much technology at your fingertips. Using that to best serve you, to protect you, is an advantage a lot of people haven't had until recent years. Every time you communicate with your landlord, property manager, or maintenance technician, make sure you have a written document of it. While having a conversation with them on the phone or in person might be important for building personal relationships, it won't help you in a court of law. Protect yourself by following up with an email, a text, or a written document. This will best serve you if something goes awry later on in the relationship. In the written document, detail where you were, when you had the conversation, who you spoke with, and what was said in the conversation. I'll go over this again when you learn more about making work order requests, but it can't be said enough!

NORMAL WEAR AND TEAR VS. DAMAGES

Normal wear and tear is simply what happens when someone lives in a space over time. Examples of normal wear and tear are warped door and window frames, sun-faded blinds and window coverings, wobbly door handles, and other things that can be taken care of or replaced easily. Even scuffs on walls and doors are normal wear and tear. It becomes property damage when you're talking about pet stains, burns, holes in walls, and broken doors, windows, porcelain, etc. It's important to understand the difference between broken or damaged items and normal wear and tear to protect yourself so you're not held responsible for things that would wear down naturally over time.

Blinds, cheap metals, and other builder-grade materials can also get damaged easily over time. Because of this, one thing to be mindful of is using items the way they were intended to be used. If you're using your bathtub faucet to help pull yourself up or using your towel rack to stabilize yourself, things like that aren't going to hold up over time. So using the things in your home the way they were intended can help make them last.

It's also common for kitchens to have tile and gloss or semi-gloss paint coats to make them easy to clean. If you have a painted wall that's a lower gloss, like eggshell or satin, it might be in your best interest to put up a temporary backsplash or contact paper in your kitchen to help prevent it from getting damaged.

Keeping your home maintained is going to help prevent larger maintenance problems down the line. Regular cleaning, decluttering, and storage options will cut down on the damage caused by dirt, pests, and other things, like mold and mildew.

Standards can be different in different states, cities, and counties when it comes to what's normal vs. what's damage. It's important to know, though, that no matter where you are in the country, no landlord can charge for normal wear and tear. But what constitutes normal wear and tear is often argued.

Landlords will look at this as trying to protect their investment. While you're having a relationship with the landlord, you need to understand you're having a relationship with someone who might view the property being more important than you. It's hard to have these discussions, but it's so critical. It doesn't mean landlords aren't reasonable people—they can't be kind—or they don't want to take care of you. They'll just protect their investment above all else.

That's why it's important to protect yourself, have plans in place, have contact with tenant resources ahead of time, and know the laws in your area. Yes, this is your home; yes, this is your safe space; but it's also important to remember that legally, these properties are owned by other people and they'll protect their interests just as you have to protect yours.

Handy Ma'am Tip:

If you use really strong peel-and-stick tiles, just know that in high-heat areas, the adhesive is going to heat up over and over and adhere more to the wall, which could damage the wall when you remove the tiles. Using a more temporary adhesive tile will be best around stoves and ovens.

Emotional Reset

People always ask me why I focus so much on renters. They ask me why I don't focus on homeowners. Supposedly, that's where the money's at, I'm told. The reality is this: I've never been a homeowner. But I've been a renter my entire adulthood.

I've lived in dorms, I've moved 10 times over seven years, and I was houseless for six months. I lived in the back of my car, I lived with friends, and, ultimately, I squatted at an apartment and I stayed there for several months until I forced the hand of the landlord, who gave me a lease—and I still live there. I've been living in that same apartment for seven years now.

When people ask why I focus on renters, the truth of the matter is because I am one. I speak from the heart and with passion. I'm just as scared of landlords and property managers as so many of you are who are reading this right now. I've worked in this field as a maintenance technician because I felt like I could help people in the field who felt like me. There were often times I bent the rules to take care of others. But all that was working within a system that was already broken.

When I'm writing these chapters and I'm thinking about how to help you, I'm reminded that the system doesn't have our best interests at heart. It has the best interests of other people who have deeper pockets than us and that's hard for me because I know how that can feel hopeless at times.

Legally, a landlord can tell you what you can and can't do in the home, but there are things they should also do for you that often don't get done. Repairs are often ignored or delayed. In a perfect world, landlords would work with you, alongside you, and empower and enlist you to take care of the property they supposedly care so much about. But they have to realize it's your home. It might be where you work, where you raise your kids, where you've shared experiences with a loved one, where you grieve the death of someone in your life you care so deeply about.

These apartments aren't just someone else's property—they're your memory, your nostalgia, your love, your passion. It's important for others to remember that if they ignore your emotions and experiences when you're speaking about a rental property simply because you don't own it yourself, then they're missing the point. These are our homes and that's why I speak up for renters, that's why I speak for renters, that's why I focus on renters.

A focus isn't an exclusion and there's no reason why a homeowner couldn't use this knowledge. There's no reason why homeowners who might become landlords someday couldn't use this knowledge for good and help other people achieve safety and comfort in their home. Housing is and should be a human right, but so many times, in a legal sense, it's not considered that. That isn't just. It's an awful oversight and a deliberate construct of those in power and it's something people don't even bat an eye at.

The number of renters is growing in our country, and while it's growing, problems and more problems will continue to arise within this system. All I want to do is fix your home for you—to help give you the tools that can guide you through these tough moments. If you don't have proper running water in your home, if you have a hole that you've been staring at for six months, if you have a wobbly door handle in your home, none of that should be ignored by the landlord. But if you have the right tools and knowledge, I'm giving you the possibility of taking care of it yourself if you see fit because you deserve to feel safe and comfortable in your home. You're worth the time it takes to learn a new skill.

3

REQUESTING A REPAIR

WHAT'S A WORK ORDER?

In an ideal world, things that are broken will be repaired. But when we're living on someone else's property, that could be much more of a hurdle. It's important to understand how you can reach out to a landlord or property manager to get the job done properly and quickly. I'm going to lay out the steps for how to make sure these work orders get addressed and then the rest of the book will entail how to be able to take care of these problems yourself if the landlord chooses not to do the work properly or in a timely fashion.

A work order is a maintenance request on behalf of yourself or someone else who lives in an apartment to a property manager or landlord. It consists of many things, but it's all going to be dictated by what's in your lease. If your lease says the landlord or property manager is responsible for replacing light bulbs, then they have to fulfill that request. If it says they're responsible for repairing all damage inside the property, then they're the ones who are liable to make sure those things are done. But some leases will also put a lot on you. This can vary depending on your county, city, or state, and it could be a minefield to try to navigate.

But for all intents and purposes, the work orders and maintenance requests I'm going to talk about will consist of everything that's in your lease and in your apartment.

The types of work orders include:

- **General maintenance:** These are things that occur most often and are non-emergencies, such as low water pressure in your sink, a clog, drywall repair, repairing the doors, appliance maintenance, and more.
- **Emergency repairs:** These include flooding caused by a clog, a sparking electrical outlet, a nonfunctional appliance (such as a fridge), or a repair for another component on the property that's required for safety and security.

Legally, your landlord is required to provide you with a home that's habitable, make necessary repairs, conduct regular maintenance, and provide you with safety and security. When you sign your lease, you should also be provided with a few things to make sure your home is safe and habitable:

- Emergency contacts and an explanation of what constitutes an emergency.
- Outline of the process for reporting any maintenance concerns.
- Your property manager's contact information.

Handy Ma'am Tip:

If you don't know the name of something, you can search Google Images to pull up a picture and descriptions of what you're looking for. This is a great tool for people who may be new to DIY or new to things like this and might not know the name of certain items. Google Images isn't always perfect, but it can put you in the right direction when you're helping the technician understand what your problem is.

HOW TO SUBMIT A WORK ORDER

How to submit a work order should be very straightforward, right? You can call your landlord or property manager, you can email them, or you can even use an online web portal that allows you to submit it directly. And if they're really old school, sometimes they do a letter submission form you can drop off at your leasing office to get the work done.

With all that being said, I'm going to talk about the best way to make sure the work gets done. No matter what, you want to make sure you get everything in writing. If you speak to someone directly or you call them, get it written down as soon as possible. An email is the best way to make sure you have a track record of what you're requesting.

A portal is the second-best way if it's available to you. A portal can often keep and maintain your requests and conversations so you know what work request you submitted and that can help keep everything documented in case they don't get the work done.

When following up in writing, summarize the conversation you had and thank them for listening to you or for agreeing to do the work. Whatever they might have said in your conversation also needs to be included. If they continue to call you regarding your request, always follow up with something in writing. It's in their best interest to have a conversation with you over the phone or in person—although it's not in your best interest. Sending that email directly after talking to them protects you and keeps everything in writing so they're legally bound to complete the request in a timely manner.

It's also important when you're filing a request that you understand how a maintenance request is received from a maintenance technician. They have to follow fair housing laws in the United States. These fair housing laws require maintenance technicians to work in the order in which they received the request unless something's considered an emergency.

It doesn't work in order of convenience or in order of what works best for the technician. It's what order it was received in. So if they get a maintenance request from somebody at 9 a.m. for a closet door that's off its tracks and then a maintenance request at 9:15 a.m. for a clogged toilet, even though the clogged toilet seems like a higher priority, legally they have to address the closet first.

You could argue that the clogged toilet is more of an emergency, but it does kind of fall in that gray area. So understanding that helps you when you file the request, making sure to put an emphasis on what's happening and how it's interfering with your daily life.

If you put in a request for a clogged toilet, note if that clogged toilet is overflowing, how much it's overflowing, and what kind of damage it's causing. This could bump it up from a regular request to an emergency, which requires an immediate response. You have to understand that a human is reading the requests and a human has to make those snap judgment decisions while they're filing the orders. The more information you can give, the better.

Having a well-described list of what's happening is also helpful in other ways. For example, it can be really hard if you say you're having a problem with an outlet. Just saying you have a problem with an outlet isn't really helping the technician bring the right tools and make sure the job can get done effectively and quickly. Fully laying out the scenario is key:

- Is nothing staying plugged in?
- Is there no power or current running through the outlets?
- Does it spark when you turn on something that's plugged in?
- Is it very loose, like the outlet itself is just shaking?

The answers to those questions are critical to provide to the maintenance technician. They'll help them do their job more effectively and quickly.

WHAT TO DO IF A WORK REQUEST IS IGNORED

Knowing what to do if your request gets ignored isn't easy. You need to first understand your local laws before taking the correct action.

Every single area is going to have a different procedure, but if you document everything in an email or written document of some kind, you'll have a better chance of making sure they get this work done effectively and sooner rather than later. If a work order isn't completed in a timely manner, which is very subjective, then you can go through the legal system to get that work done.

But always know you're dealing with a human on the other side, and if you hurt the relationship with how you go about a work request, it can sometimes make your living situation even harder. Moving can be expensive and hard, so proceed with caution and do the best you can to navigate this. I also want you to know you're not alone—a lot of people go through this and it can be very frustrating.

EMERGENCY REQUESTS

Knowing the difference between what's simply a request and what's an emergency is also important. A maintenance emergency can consist of one of the following:

- No heat during freezing weather
- No air conditioning in hot weather
- A broken lock on your door
- A broken or leaking gas line
- Flooding or a broken water line
- A fire
- A break-in or security breach

Keep in mind that your maintenance technician isn't going to be able to put out a fire or turn the lights back on if an entire grid system has lost power. But you should still file a work order so the request is documented.

What's an emergency from a legal perspective is different depending on where you live. A lot of states have a very clear definition of what's an emergency request and the laws surrounding those types of requests. Document all that so you know what kind of request you're dealing with if inaction becomes a problem, such as your landlord taking 48 hours to repair something that's really crucial, like heat during a winter storm, or taking more than a month to repair something you requested, which could be negligence. All that's going to be clearly defined in your state law.

WHAT TO DO IF YOUR EMERGENCY REQUEST IS IGNORED

When it comes to one of the emergencies mentioned here, most states do have laws that require the work to be done immediately, and if not, there could be a lawsuit. If you've documented everything as suggested, you can encourage your landlord to act by setting a deadline for the work to be completed. Let them know that if the work hasn't been done by this time, you'll take further action.

You can:

- Call the city's local building inspector and request they inspect the building. They can help with certain emergencies, such as lack of heat or hot water, a pest infestation, water damage, or mold, but not cosmetic things, such as faded paint or stained carpeting. The building inspector can order the landlord to make the repairs by a deadline and they'll come back to see that the repairs have been completed.
- If there's no local inspector, you can call the fire department, public health inspector, or a Department of Safety.

In most places, it's illegal for the landlord to retaliate against you for asserting your rights. You also shouldn't be charged for more damage that's caused by lack of action on the landlord's part.

You can even potentially withhold the rent for the month until the work is done. Check for the rent abatement laws in your area because this isn't legal in every state and needs to be something you look into before withholding rent.

Some areas don't allow you to withhold rent, but you can request rent abatement, where you'd get rent credit when the landlord refuses to fix an issue that affects your health and safety or your ability to live in the home.

In the most dire circumstances, you might even be able to move out and be relieved of your lease because the landlord was unable to provide you with a habitable home. If you find yourself in any of these difficult situations, please contact your local tenant resources group as soon as possible. Most areas have them.

Emotional Reset

In an ideal world, you'd never have to use any of the repair tutorials in this book if you're a renter. In an ideal world, you don't need this book at all, but we don't live in an ideal world. We live in a world where people don't uphold their promises and sometimes don't do the work we believe they should be doing.

This is your home. You deserve to feel safe in your home and to have it be functional. If the home isn't living up to those standards, then you need to take matters into your own hands. There are things you should be aware of, but I don't want to put you in a dangerous or uncomfortable position. But if you know you can do this work and all you need is a little encouragement and step-by-step instructions to make sure you do it properly, then this book will help.

A lot of people are going to look at this book and tell you they don't like that this exists. They won't like that this book sits on a shelf and tells a renter to do work that their landlord is supposed to be doing. My response to that is: If landlords upheld their promises and upheld what they said they'd do, then you'd never have to use this book.

But because bad landlords exist and because people don't always uphold their promises, we need to sometimes take care of each other. Especially in the LGBTQIA+ community and other marginalized communities. We're often the ones who are most vulnerable when broken promises happen. So just remember that if you're doing this work, it's not right and it isn't fair, but I'm proud of you for taking the steps you need to get the work done, documenting everything, and protecting your home and everyone inside it. You're doing a great job and I'm extremely proud of you.

4

TROUBLESHOOTING

BEING A DETECTIVE

A cornerstone of maintenance work is troubleshooting and that can entail a lot of different things. The reason why it's such an important attribute to consider when approaching any type of home repair is that you can often solve major problems by simply catching something early. Knowing what things could occur and understanding a basic approach to fixing them can help keep you from getting discouraged.

Having a blueprint to process how to repair and maintain something will keep you moving forward in your learning. This particular blueprint is a technique I've used in my own work over the last 15 years. I've used it during particularly trying times—when the anxiety of even approaching the work was so overwhelming.

I call this approach for identifying and tackling difficult issues "The Mercury Method." First of all, don't assume you know all the answers to the problem based on previous experiences. I want you to put away your previous experiences with things and look at this new experience for what it is—an opportunity to learn.

For example, if there's a clog in the toilet and toilet paper has always been the culprit, I want you to just push that to the side and really look at what the problems are. Are there air bubbles popping up? Is this something that's been dislodged a few times when flushing? Or is this something that's occurred slowly over time?

Really take a look at what's in front of you because it could be something different, like a stuck toy. If you apply the same method you've used before for unclogging the toilet, you might jam the toy so far down into the S-trap of the toilet that you may have to get a new toilet. I've been there.

You want to make sure you're stopping the actual problem, not just a symptom of the problem. Maybe you're seeing a flickering light in the hallway, so you replace that bulb, but what you're not realizing is that the switch is pretty gummy. The switch is actually causing this problem, but you just assumed right away it must be the light bulb. In this case, you're not **really** solving the problem—you're just giving the appearance of solving the problem.

I also want you to keep something in the back of your mind: safety. Is it appropriate for you to do the work or should you bring in a professional? Remember that when you're taking on home improvement issues, you should never work outside your comfort zone. Be mindful that yes, you can do all the work that's in this book, but first, truly ask yourself if you're capable of doing so at this moment or if it would be best for you to ask for help.

THE MERCURY METHOD

The Mercury Method consists of five major steps:

- Identify
- Eliminate
- Source
- Plan
- Breathe

No matter what the genre of the issue is—from electrical and plumbing to painting and drywall repair—remembering to identify, eliminate, source, plan, and breathe will help keep you grounded throughout the process. This work can be overwhelming and it can make you feel like there's no way you could possibly get through it, but stick with the method and you'll be fine.

IDENTIFY

The first step in the process is to identify the issue. For example, let's say you have a door that won't close all the way. That's the issue—the door getting stuck on the trim. It's not the latch malfunctioning or the door being loose. The door is getting stuck at the top of the door trim.

Once you've identified the issue, it doesn't mean you should take action just yet. I don't want you to consider what's causing this issue at this stage—you just want to call it out. This will help you stay grounded in the process so you can later isolate what's causing the issue and fix the source of it.

ELIMINATE

The next step in the process is eliminate. Staying with the example of the door being stuck at the top of the trim, consider what all the causes could be and rule out what you know for sure it's not. You're going to look at the big picture **and** the details to uncover what's really happening—check out every aspect of the door; see if there's a transition pad on the floor that's a little too high and pushing the door up; look at the door hinges to see if they're all nice and tight; check that the trim of the door is even by using a 90° triangle ruler to see how flush everything is. Looking into all the possibilities will help solve the problem.

Once each possibility has been eliminated, you should be left with either one or two possible routes to go. Remember that this is sometimes a little bit of a guessing game, especially with something like plumbing, when you can't always see what's happening. Make your best guess and go with the option that's going to be the least damaging.

Sticking with the door example, I don't want you to have to cut the door to get it to close properly. There are typically other things you can do, such as working with the hinge pins, that don't cause long-term ramifications for the door. So when it comes to eliminating, it's always best to go with the route that's going to be the path of least resistance. If you try that and it doesn't work, you move on to the next one.

SOURCE

Source and Eliminate tend to work in tandem. The process of elimination will lead you to the source of the issue. Once you know the source, you can test it out to make sure it's the only source of the problem. For the door example, say you've eliminated every possible issue and what's left is a bent hinge pin. That's the source of the problem.

You can sometimes see the source and verify it. Other times, you have to make the best determination you can with the information you have. Know that this is okay—you don't have to do this perfectly and you don't have to be right all the time. You just have to understand you need to ground yourself and not jump to conclusions.

If you think the source is something like, "The door is just too big for this opening. I must cut down this door," that's a huge task to take on—and what if you're wrong? If you jump steps and you go past other possible sources instead of taking it one step at a time, you could cause more issues down the road. So remember to look for the source and go for the solution that's going to give you the best chance of being successful at the time.

PLAN

This next step is one of the most important ones and should never be overlooked. Plan a strategy to contain the problem—that's what you're aiming for here. You're not always looking to solve the problem outright, but you're doing the best you can to make it better, so you want to make sure it doesn't get any worse.

While you're planning, you might realize you missed something and have to reassess the situation. That's completely normal. It's okay to do the best you can and then redo something or go back to step 1. You can identify, eliminate, source, and then plan again when needed. This format—these five steps you keep circling back to—will keep you grounded and safe as you're trying various solutions.

If you replace the hinge pin and the door is still catching up top, then the next step might be to take a planer and sand the top of the door at the stress point. But you don't want to skip the steps to fix the pins first and you don't want to skip the steps to assess the hinges. You want to make sure before you get to the major projects that you're taking things slowly and step-by-step.

And I can't stress this enough: The best-laid plans are often thrown away when you encounter new problems. You might try something, and during that process, you identify another issue you weren't aware of, so the whole process should start over again. Once you encounter something you didn't know previously, you need to go back and identify, eliminate, source, and plan again.

BREATHE

This is the last step in the process. Making space for yourself to breathe allows you to learn effectively. When you're approaching these problems, you're often stressed out already. You have this problem that's likely been going on for a long time and you've just been living with it because you didn't know there was another route to go. Or you know this is going to cost a lot of money and you're stretching your skills to the limit to save some costs. All these things can be really hard, so I want you to take space for yourself.

I know you can do this. I know you're going to be okay. And I know that deep down, you know that too. But when you're in this process and you're identifying, isolating, sourcing, and then planning, you can get stuck in all that and you don't remember to breathe. Nothing will get done effectively if you're so tense you're shaking and you're not breathing. And if you're not breathing, then you're not thinking. If you're rushing a job, I can almost guarantee the job will end poorly.

The jobs I regret the most, the jobs I have fallen short on as a technician, are the ones where I didn't make space for myself to fail. You think of failing as the end of everything—like it's the worst thing that could happen—and honestly, sometimes it can be, but failing is ultimately not a bad thing. There are so many lessons and so many things you learn from failing that I've learned to value my failures more than my successes. It might sound cliché, but failures are important for education and learning. I'm happy you're taking a moment to breathe and remembering that you're worth the time it takes to learn a new skill.

Emotional Reset

Troubleshooting is so overlooked that many people try to jump right to the solutions that others have given. When your car breaks down and doesn't start, you can always guarantee someone's going to say the battery is dead or the alternator isn't working. That's great, but it's ignoring all the other possibilities.

There's a lot that goes into your home—there are a lot of things that are connected to each other. And if you make assumptions, you could be missing the problem entirely. As a technician in this field for 15 years, I can tell you this can happen to the best of us. So remember to take time and make space for this process because this process will keep you from drowning in the sea of possibilities.

All this is one step at a time. All you're doing is building new skills and new ways of looking at things. These steps can help you approach things in a more effective way for yourself. Because you don't know what you don't know! If you're doing something for the very first time, how could you possibly know the problems that could occur? If you're doing drywall for the first time, how would you ever know that bubbles could be created?

So don't beat yourself up with all the information you don't know because, as I said, you don't know what you don't know. And if you don't know, you can't do anything to prevent it. Keep doing the best you can with the information you have. Breathe along the way. Just approaching all this and reading this chapter shows you're ready to do this work! This chapter might not be the most glamorous and it might not even be the reason why you bought this book, but this chapter is a cornerstone to the whole process. This is the part you can come back to and remind yourself it's possible. Keep reminding yourself you can do this—one step at a time.

5

BUILDING A TOOLKIT

NOT TOO MANY TOOLS

The backbone of every how-to book is the tool section. Often authors in this field will tell you how to use every tool under the sun. They want you to be prepared for any project or any task you may encounter. But often, that can leave us overwhelmed and sometimes even confused. It can also be nearly impossible for many of us to even afford most of the tools they list in these sections.

I know you likely aren't a professional who'll be doing any of these tasks for years to come or probably even someone who looks at themselves as a home renovator. And with all that in mind, I want to work within your budget and within the tasks you're truly setting out to accomplish. The best tools for you are going to be the ones that are on hand and can make you feel ready to go in a moment's notice.

The four most versatile tools that are best for maintenance and repairs are a multi-bit screwdriver (at least an 11-in-1), a utility knife, adjustable pliers, and a set of metric and standard Allen keys.

Because these are the foundation of your new tool collection, make sure to go for quality over quantity. The cheapest-quality tools often have a shorter life span. And you might end up spending more in the long run because you'll have to buy a tool multiple times over the course of months or years. So aim for buying once and buying for durability so they can support the weight of being foundational tools in your tool kit.

You can usually spot a low-quality tool by its cost. Tools aren't cheap to make, and if they are, it's often because they're using plastic pieces to substitute for more expensive metal components. And if they're metal, they'll often have hollow cores that are poorly created that could break at the most inconvenient time. It's also worth noting that if they're tools like screwdrivers and Allen keys, they don't always correctly fit the slots they were created for. Lower-quality tools are also often lighter than their more expensive siblings. Quality tools are also often designed for comfort, like a handle that doesn't make your hand cramp up, which is often well worth the investment.

"In this book, I'm going to focus on the most versatile tools you'll use for the majority of the tasks in your home. They won't always be the perfect tool designed for that specific task, but they'll be the ones that will get the job done most effectively and economically."

All that being said, if there's a financial hurdle for you and you can't invest in more expensive versions of these four tools, that's okay. Having any version of these tools is better than not having them at all. And I don't want the cost to add to the stress or tension you might feel about these tasks. Just be aware that some caution might be required—and a little extra patience.

MULTI-BIT SCREWDRIVER (11-IN-1)

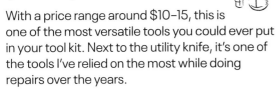

With a price range around $10–15, this is one of the most versatile tools you could ever put in your tool kit. Next to the utility knife, it's one of the tools I've relied on the most while doing repairs over the years.

This one tool has 11 interchangeable components and it can be so less stressful to have one tool instead of having a tool kit full of tools. The more tools you have, the more likely the chance you'll lose some of them before you need to use them.

This screwdriver will have ³⁄₁₆ and ¼ slots for a flathead screwdriver, #1 and #2 sizes for a Phillips screwdriver, T10 and T12 torque bits (otherwise known as a star bit), #1 and #2 square bits (becoming more and more common), and even a nut driver, which is used for a lot of appliances or furniture assembly, for ¼, ⁵⁄₁₆, and ³⁄₈ nuts.

The multi-bit screwdrivers I'd focus on are the ones where the bits are all kept in the barrel of the screwdriver instead of on the top of the handle or in a separate case. If they're in the barrel, I've noticed I'm more likely to not lose them before the job is done or even before the job starts.

Some brands I recommend are Klein, Milwaukee, Lenox, and Husky.

UTILITY KNIFE

This tool is not just one of the handiest tools I've ever had (and will cost you a mere $10–20), but it's also the tool I use the most outside of any maintenance needs. It's the tool I'll grab when I need to open something and to feel safe walking around in my everyday life. And that's good, but it also means I often don't have it when I need it because I misplace it so often. So if you know you'll be like me and use it for things outside of maintenance, get yourself two of them and label one "Repairs ONLY." Little things like that help a great deal.

That being said, box cutters are nice but not ideal for most repairs and maintenance needs. A knife can be used to scrap something, to cut, to poke, or to sharpen things. It's such a handy tool in those moments that it just simply can't be overlooked. Bonus points if the knife has a jagged edge because you can use it as a miniature saw in a pinch—and that feature has saved me many times. It can cut PVC pipe and wood, and if you have a limited number of tools, it's totally one of the tools worth having.

Brands I recommend are DeWalt, Milwaukee, and Gerber.

ADJUSTABLE PLIERS (12-INCH [30.5CM])

One of the reasons why I avoid a store-bought, pre-assembled tool kit is because it leaves out the adjustable pliers (which will cost you $15–30). I don't know why this is. Maybe it's because it's hard to create this tool cheaply and have it be functional. But few tools are as necessary as this gem. It's absolutely required for nearly all plumbing jobs, plus it can be used in most instances where you'd use a crescent wrench or slip-joint pliers. It does cost more and I wouldn't buy a cheap one if you can avoid it. The best kinds are ones that have some type of locking mechanism that allows the jaws to stay put when you're using the pliers without them coming undone.

Brands I recommend and Irwin, Channellock, and Doyle.

ALLEN KEYS (METRIC AND STANDARD)

Allen keys are most commonly used to assemble and repair appliances, furniture, and plumbing, but they're very important tools to have on hand for lots of other purposes. Having a standard set (in inches) and a metric set (each costing you $10–25) will ensure you have an Allen key for any situation. This way, you'll be prepared and won't be elbows deep into a repair and realize you don't have the Allen key you need.

Having a set of Allen keys that's attached to a folding mechanism is my preferred kind because it's much harder to lose the keys. And when you have something you invest in like this,

you want to make sure you always have what you need when you need it. So reducing the possibility that you could have parts go missing is critical to success.

Brands I recommend are Craftsman, Eklind, and Stanley.

WHERE ARE THE HAMMER AND TAPE MEASURE?!?

I hear this all the time, but remember the purpose for this tool kit—for maintenance and repairs—and a hammer is rarely useful for these types of tasks. And to be honest, I trust a piece of string or nylon rope over most tape measures because I'm dyslexic. That's not to say these aren't helpful. They absolutely are. But when you're starting out, it's nice to focus on what will help you the most with repairs.

That's only to say that the next tools to get other than the fundamental four would be a hammer, flashlight, and tape measure. For most home needs, you won't need anything fancy in a hammer and a lightweight 8-ounce mini hammer will do just fine if you're on a budget. Plus, you might want something that can fit nicely and compactly in a storage location.

A good tape measure for your needs is usually 25 feet (7.6m) long. Always get something with clear markings to make it easier to understand if you need that, like I do.

Flashlights will be great in an emergency situation if the power goes out, or if you need to see into dark spaces, under cabinets, in closets, etc. Just a regular flashlight with backup batteries will be good in most situations.

OTHER TOOLS AND MATERIALS

As you go on this home repair journey together, you'll need to get some tools that are not yet listed as well as materials needed to get a job done. I'll list them all here with a brief description to help you on your way. As you do more and more specialized tasks, your tool collection will also grow more and more.

PLUMBING TOOLS

Squeezable tube of silicone caulking: This is the best for sealing fixtures and joints to prevent water or air from going in or out.

Plumbers grease: A type of grease that lubricates and protects plumbing materials, such as taps and valve stems.

Threaded tape: Mainly used for water connections to provide a tight seal.

Drain auger or Snake: Hand augers are good for sink and tub clogs.

DRYWALL TOOLS

6-inch Joint knife: Ideal for spreading spackling paste and drywall joint compound.

Joint compound: Drywall mud or just mud. It consists mainly of gypsum and limestone and is used in putting up walls or making repairs in drywall.

Mesh tape: An adhesive material used for jointing and reinforcing drywall.

2-inch Putty knife: Helps you spread joint compound, spackle, or adhesive.

12-inch Mud pan: Great for holding and mixing joint compound (mud).

5-minute Drywall powder: Easy Sand has a 5-minute working time before it begins to harden. It is ideal for small repairs such as nail holes.

PAINTING TOOLS

9-inch Roller and roller cover: Used to apply paint to walls for large areas. The "nap" is the thickness of the roller cover and will vary depending on the paint job you're doing.

Paint pail: A handy paint pail can hold your paint and brush for small projects like painting around trim and ceilings.

5 x 5-foot Canvas with plastic underneath: A drop cloth helps to protect your floors during painting projects, and the plastic underneath will prevent damage to your floors from spills.

3-inch Angled nylon brush: Great for trim, moldings, doors, or other small jobs.

Paint tray: For your rollers to help you get a smooth application.

FrogTape or painter's tape: For taping edges, windows, frames, and along walls where you do not want paint to go.

Shortcut brush: Best brush for cutting in along ceilings, corners, trim, doors, and windows.

ELECTRICAL TOOLS

Insulated screwdriver: Insulated handles are rubber and can protect you from electric shock when working with electricity.

Insulated wire strippers/ cutters: Helps you to strip the casing off wires to expose the wire, or used as cutters to trim wire.

Wire nuts: Place and twist over wires that you connect together to keep the connection safe and secure.

Emotional Reset

Gatekeeping knowledge often comes with a price tag or with words like, "You must have the right tool for the job." If you stick to that notice too tightly, it can restrict you from attempting to repair things around you.

The truth is, the best tools are the ones you have on hand because you can accomplish amazing things with patience, determination, and faith in yourself. Trust yourself with growing that tool kit over time, but don't allow others' words to stand in your way of the things you need to feel safe and secure in your home.

Tools should be an extension of your mind. They should help you along on your hero's quest, not prohibit you or make your task harder. Think of these as your Excalibur or as your lightsaber that defends you from sudden moments of uncertainty and gives you confidence when problems arise. I'm proud of you for getting the things you need before problems occur, saving you from stress later and definitely giving you the peace of mind you deserve.

PART 2

★

MAKING REPAIRS

BATHROOM FAUCETS AND DRAINS

THE DREADED, NO GOOD, STINKY CLOG

First things first: I know this is an overwhelming and gross topic for some. Disgusting clogs are a real possibility when removing a block in your drains, but prolonging the issue or ignoring it altogether can lead to something much worse than a clog—and that's sewage backup! So if you're completely grossed out by hair, grime, and wet objects, I suggest getting a face mask, safety glasses, and some work gloves. Protective equipment can help the process be at least a little less terrible and make this task more possible for you.

Second, don't be upset with yourself, no matter what you find. Large clumps of hair and other buildup are totally natural and nothing to be ashamed of. Have children and find toys that went mysteriously missing long ago? Trust me, it's very common and you aren't a terrible parent if this happens. Several years ago, when I was working with a great crew of plumbers, we were discussing our largest nightmare finds in plumbing. Mine was pedestrian compared with some of the horrors I heard. But not one of them was upset about hair, toys, or other natural blockages. Their idea of a bad clog included underwear, shoes, and baseball caps being found in drains. So rest assured that feeling bad about your clogs isn't a necessary requirement when doing plumbing.

UNCLOGGING A DRAIN CLOG IN A BATHROOM SINK

Words to Know:

Overflow drain: This secondary drain helps prevent an overflow or flooding by giving another exit path for the water.

P-trap: This piping arrangement traps water to help prevent sewage from backing into your drains.

WHAT NOT TO DO

- Don't use chemicals first. Use them as a last resort. (See page 71.)
- Avoid plastic drain snakes because they can break off in your drain and cause a much larger problem.
- Air carriage plungers can also dislodge pipes and cause leaks.
- Never use home remedies you find on the internet, like depilatories that thin out hair on your body, to remove a clog. These can harm your pipes and cause more damage long term.

DIAGNOSING THE PROBLEM

Run the water to see how long it takes for the clog to back up the drain. Be sure to time this because it will help later.

- If it takes a few seconds, the problem might be directly under the stopper or inside the P-trap.
- If it takes 30 seconds or more, the clog might be farther down the drainpipe and might require a drain snake rather than other methods.

Also, ask yourself: "When did this problem start?"

- If it's a quick, sudden clog, it's likely a toy, a wad of paper, or something else that's a recent blockage and chemicals aren't going to help that anyway.
- If it was a slow accumulation over time, then it's likely something farther down the drain or just a slow buildup of sludge and debris.

TROUBLESHOOTING: WHAT'S NEXT?

If the clog is shallow and nearby, a plunger is a great first place to start. You'll want a simple sink plunger or an accordion plunger for this task. Either one will give you good suction without damaging your sink with too much power.

THE PLUNGER METHOD

MATERIALS

simple sink plunger or
accordion plunger and
a wet rag

HOW DO YOU KNOW IF IT WORKED?

Run hot water for the same amount of time and see if the sink still backs up or if it operates properly. If it takes longer to back up, part of the clog could have gone farther down the drain pipe or a second clog could have been discovered. You can repeat this method again to see if you're able to further loosen up the clog or move on to the next method.

TROUBLESHOOTING: WHAT'S NEXT?

- If the clog is still shallow, I recommend cleaning out your P-trap.

- If the clog is farther down the drain pipe, I recommend using a drain snake.

1 Remove the stopper to the drain.

2 If there's an overflow drain, make sure to cover the drain with a wet rag to get the maximum amount of suction possible when plunging.

3 Fill up the surrounding area with some water to help seal the edges of the plunger.

4 Place the plunger over the drain and plunge with the beat of a pulsating heartbeat. This movement helps loosen potential clogs.

5 Use your hand or the rag from the overflow drain to remove any debris that's pulled up.

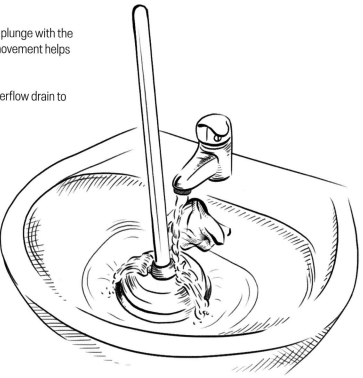

THE P-TRAP METHOD

MATERIALS

small bucket or bowl, adjustable pliers, and something to remove the clog with (a flathead screwdriver, scribe, or cleaning brush work well)

HOW DO YOU KNOW IF IT WORKED?

Run hot water for the same amount of time and see if the sink still backs up or if it operates properly. If it still backs up, it's time to use the drain snake.

TROUBLESHOOTING: WHAT'S NEXT?

- If the clog is still shallow, I recommend cleaning out your P-trap.

- If the clog is farther down the drain pipe, I recommend using a drain snake.

1 Remove anything under the sink that could be damaged by water.

2 Place a small bucket or bowl under the P-trap.

3 Use the adjustable pliers to remove both nuts holding up the P-trap.

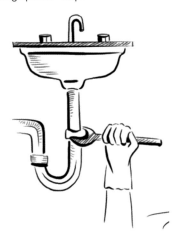

Handy Ma'am Tip:

If you've removed the P-trap and see a clog, you can use a Zip-It or another clog removal tool. As long as there's no chance of it getting broken and lost down the drain, it might help you directly reach a clog in the pipe.

7 If you find a blockage, remove it the best you can with a scribe, flathead screwdriver, or any type of cleaning brush.

8 Reattach the P-trap and be sure to not overtighten the nuts and crack them. Tighten by hand first and finish up with a half turn by the pliers.

4 Once the trap is off, look inside and check to see if there's a clog.

5 Be sure to look into the drain pipe that leads into the P-trap. There might be hair and other debris still attached, which are likely causing the clog.

6 If there's nothing that's blocking the passage, then you might need to move on to the next method before putting the P-trap back together.

9 Pour 2 cups of water down the drain to make sure the P-trap isn't leaking.

THE DRAIN SNAKE METHOD

small bowl or bucket, rag, ⅛ hand auger (drain snake), utility knife

1   If you've not already removed the P-trap, follow steps 1–3 on page 69.

2   With the trap off, place the end of the snake down the drain pipe.

   Bending the tip of the auger at a 45° angle helps get around the bend and elbows of the pipe.

3   Start with 1 foot (30.5cm) of the auger at a time, rotating it each time it goes deeper to help dislodge scraps or debris in the pipe.

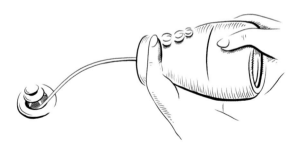

4   The closer the auger is to the opening, the easier it is to get into the pipe. If you're struggling to get it to go down into the pipe, hold the auger closer to the drain for more leverage. Keep the auger 3-7 inches (8-18cm) from the opening so you can't see the snake itself.

5   If you can see the snake start to bend around itself, there's too much snake exposed. Get it 2–3 inches (5–8cm) closer, let some snake out to push and create tension, then back off to 3-7 inches (8-18cm) again. This will usually only need to happen when the snake's trying to bend around curves.

6   Go for at least 8 feet (2.4m)—most clogs are discovered within this distance. You risk getting the auger stuck if you go too much farther.

7   Spin the auger in the opposite direction and wind it back up, making sure to clean it and wipe it down as it extracts to prevent rusting.

8   Once the tip of the auger is out, inspect any clog that might have been pulled out.

   - If it's hair, I'd advise going back down the drain with the hand auger to double check that you've gotten all of it. Hair tends to clump once it forms a clog and there might be more than one clog that's developed.

   - If you pull out another foreign object, such as a paper towel, a rag, or another object, this typically indicates a newer clog—and the clog should now be free.

   - If you pulled out nothing but the tip is dirty and appears to have scraped something, you could have still dislodged a clog and might be in the clear. It could also mean you came close to the clog but didn't reach it entirely. I'd advise going back down to be sure it's gone.

HOW DO YOU KNOW IF IT WORKED?

Run hot water for the same amount of time to see if the sink still backs up or if it operates properly. If there's still a clog, repeat this process.

TROUBLESHOOTING: WHAT'S NEXT?

You've exhausted all the previously mentioned ideas, so what do you do now? It's time to use the last resort: chemical drain cleaners. I recommend using products that are strong and industrial strength.

9   Remove the debris from the tip. A utility knife is best for this, but you can also twist it off by turning the snake in the opposite direction you used while in the drain.

10   Reattach the P-trap. Be sure to not overtighten the nuts because it's easy to crack them. Start by tightening the nuts by hand and finish with a half turn with the pliers. This should be plenty tight.

11   Pour 2 cups of water down the drain to make sure the P-trap isn't leaking.

12   Run hot water down the drain to help flush any remaining debris that might now be dislodged.

WHY DON'T I RECOMMEND CHEMICALS SOONER?

- If you rely too heavily on chemicals, it can cause long-term damage to your plumbing system. Occasional use only is recommended.

- If the chemical doesn't dissolve the clog, it can loosen the clog up slightly and cause it to go farther down your drain. This can create larger and more difficult clogs to remove.

- Your drains aren't ideal conditions for many of these chemicals to work. They're filled with moisture and grime, which dilute the chemicals and cause them to become weaker and weaker as they move down the drain.

- If used carelessly, chemicals can cause harm, so be mindful and wear personal protective equipment when you handle these products.

- The environmental impact of these harsh chemicals shouldn't be overlooked. Water-cleaning plants aren't 100% effective, so it's important to be mindful of what you put down your drains. Everyone should play their part in keeping our waterways clean.

LAST-CHANCE CHEMICALS

These chemicals are listed in no particular order. Follow the instructions on the labels for these products. Be sure to wear eye protection and gloves, and handle these chemicals with caution.

- Xion Lab

- Zep Liquid Heat

- Bio-Clean

- Thrift

- Drano Max Gel

THE NEVER-ENDING FAUCET REPAIRS

UNDERSTANDING THE PROBLEM

Your sink typically has one to two nuts that are tightened to bolts underneath your sink to hold everything in place. Think of your sink countertop as salami in between two buns, making a nice Italian sub. The faucet base is one bun and the nuts down below are the other bun. Over time, turning on the handle and putting things against the base can cause the nuts to loosen. All sink faucets are different depending on brand and model. This will lead to a variety of possible repairs. But the "Italian sub" will always be the same.

TIGHTENING A FAUCET BASE

MATERIALS

hydrogen peroxide, rag, and a basin wrench (a specialty tool that will make this process much more accessible for you)

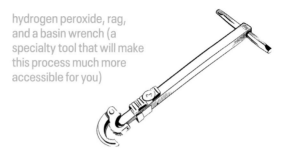

1   Identify if there's rust or calcium buildup around the nuts and bolts by looking underneath the sink.

- If there is, you're going to want to break the calcium or rust off so you can get a tighter, more snug fit.

- If rust is preventing the tightening of the nut, hydrogen peroxide will dissolve the rust . You can use a rag soaked with it or a cup filled with it to clean the nut.

- You can then use a wrench, adjustable pliers, a socket set, or a basin wrench to tighten the nut righty tighty toward the countertop.

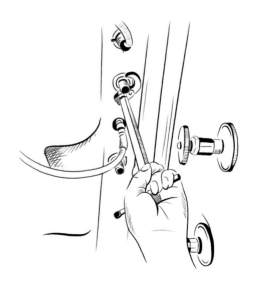

NUT SIZES & BOLT DIAMETERS (IN INCHES)

NUT SIZE	BOLT DIAMETER	
	Min (in)	Max (in)
¼	0.245	0.25
⁵⁄₁₆	0.3065	0.3125
⅜	0.369	0.375
⁷⁄₁₆	0.4305	0.4375
½	0.493	0.5
⁹⁄₁₆	0.5545	0.5625
⅝	0.617	0.625
¾	0.741	0.75
⅞	0.866	0.875
1	0.99	1
1⅛	1.114	1.125
1¼	1.239	1.25
1⅜	1.363	1.375
1½	1.488	1.5
1¾	1.738	1.75
2	1.988	2
2¼	2.238	2.25
2½	2.488	2.5
2¾	2.738	2.75
3	2.988	3

NUT SIZES & BOLT DIAMETERS (IN METRIC)

NUT SIZE	BOLT DIAMETER	
	Min (mm)	Max (mm)
M5	4.82	5
M6	5.82	6
M8	7.78	8
M10	9.78	10
M12	11.73	12
M14	13.73	14
M16	15.73	16
M18	17.73	18
M20	19.67	20
M22	21.67	22
M24	23.67	24
M27	26.67	27
M30	29.67	30
M33	32.61	33

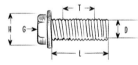

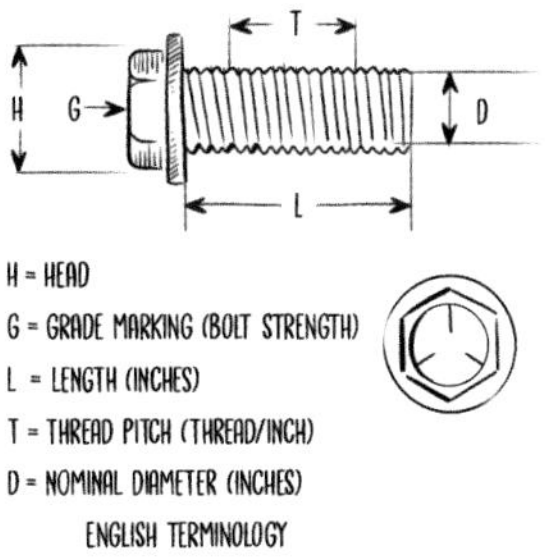

H = HEAD
G = GRADE MARKING (BOLT STRENGTH)
L = LENGTH (INCHES)
T = THREAD PITCH (THREAD/INCH)
D = NOMINAL DIAMETER (INCHES)

ENGLISH TERMINOLOGY

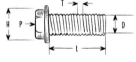

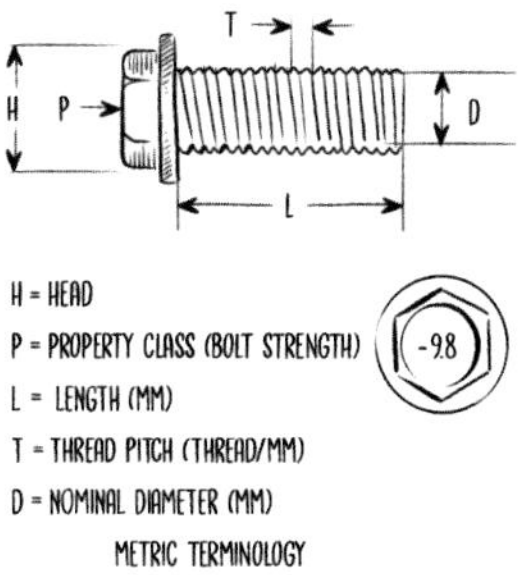

H = HEAD
P = PROPERTY CLASS (BOLT STRENGTH)
L = LENGTH (MM)
T = THREAD PITCH (THREAD/MM)
D = NOMINAL DIAMETER (MM)

METRIC TERMINOLOGY

2   If there's a missing nut or there was no nut to begin with, you can measure the bolt to find the size of nut you need.

- Use a ruler, measuring tape, or another measuring tool to measure the diameter of the bottom of the bolt to determine the nut size needed.

- Bolt diameter is measured as a straight line along the bottom of the bolt from thread to thread. See the D in the diagram.

FINAL STEPS

Once you've replaced or tightened up the nuts underneath the sink, you can go back to the faucet. To be safe, let's add some silicone caulking around the base of the faucet. This will help keep it in place just a little more in the future. Make sure to apply it smoothly around and wet your finger to smooth out the silicone. Allow the caulk to dry and cure before use (typically a few hours).

REPAIRING LOW WATER PRESSURE IN A SINK

What an annoying problem low water press is—sometimes it's so subtle, you might not see it with your eyes, but once the water hits your skin, you sure can. There are several routes to repair this problem. I'll start with the accessible one and work toward more complicated repairs.

DIAGNOSING THE PROBLEM

- Is the pressure the same regardless of whether the water is hot or cold? If yes, then the aerator is where I'd recommend starting.
- Is the pressure lower when it's hot or cold but not the other? If yes, then skip ahead to replacing the supply line.
- Is it consistently low pressure all throughout the house?

Handy Ma'am Tip:

If your water pressure is low all throughout the house, there's usually a larger issue that will need to be addressed by your landlord—almost always with the hot water heater tank. Unfortunately, there's not much you can do if it's the whole house.

Words to Know:

Faucet aerator: This mechanical device is used to reduce the amount of splashing from faucets. It's also used to conserve water and energy.

Supply line: This is the water line connected to your faucet underneath the sink—often detachable from the rest.

Faucet cartridge: This controls the flow of the water—located underneath the handle—usually hot and cold water.

Faucet stem: This controls the flow of the water—located underneath the handle. There will be either a hot water stem or a cold water stem under each handle.

THE FAUCET AERATOR

CLEANING THE AERATOR

This is the quickest solution out of this trio of possibilities. Faucet aerators have a filter in them and that little dude can surely collect friends pretty quickly. No worry though—you don't even need to take off the aerator to clean this device.

MATERIALS

toothbrush, rag, vinegar, compact mirror

1 Soak the rag in vinegar and hold it up to the tip of the faucet and rub it into the aerator. Repeat a few times. This will loosen up and dissolve some of the particles.

2 Dip the toothbrush into the vinegar and scrub the aerator.

3 A compact mirror will help you see the aerator. You'll want to see as much debris removed as possible.

4 Turn on the faucet to see if water flow has improved.

5 If results aren't ideal, then you might want to remove the aerator and soak it in vinegar.

REPLACING THE AERATOR

Faucet aerators can be found at an affordable price at nearly any hardware store. Some faucet brands and models will have one built inside the unit that might not be replaceable without changing out the entire faucet. But the majority of what you'll see in an apartment will have replaceable aerators.

MATERIALS

rag, adjustable pliers

1 Place the rag on the aerator and then the teeth of the pliers on the rag.

2 Squeeze the pliers tightly and turn the aerator lefty loosey.

3 Inspect the old aerator for damage or if it was severely clogged. (Knowing why the aerator is causing the low pressure will help prevent the problem from happening again.)

4 Place the new aerator into the faucet and tighten by hand it until it's snug.

5 Place the rag and pliers on the new aerator and tighten it righty tighty.

6 Slowly turn the faucet on to see if the pressure has improved.

REPLACING THE SUPPLY LINES

If you've done all the previous procedures and the results were the same, then it's time to move on to the next possibilities. Don't be discouraged by this. The process of elimination is a part of this journey and I'm proud of you for staying with it and learning as you go.

- The supply lines are located underneath the sink. There's one supply line for the hot water and one for the cold. If your hot water is lower pressure than your cold water, this might be one of the two most common possibilities.

  - Take the supply line off and try to bend it to look inside. You can usually see or feel that it's clogged because it's full of debris or won't bend.

  - I'd then suggest replacing the one supply line that corresponds to low pressure in the sink.

Handy Ma'am Tip:

If you're having trouble finding which supply line is hot and which is cold, a little trick that can help is turn on the hot water until it's warm and then touch both supply lines. The warmer one is the hot water supply line and the other is the cold water supply line. You can purchase a new supply from any hardware store. Try to match the length of the current one if possible.

MATERIALS

bucket, adjustable pliers, rag

1 Turn off the hot/cold water valve. Double check that it's off by turning on the faucet.

2 Place a bucket under the supply line to collect leftover water from the supply line and spigot.

3 Use adjustable pliers to turn the nut to loosen the supply line from the valve.

4 Use the pliers to loosen the supply line directly from the faucet.

5 Connect the new supply line to the valve spigot and tighten it up with pliers. (Use a rag to prevent damage to the nut.)

6 Connect the other side of the new supply line to the faucet spigot and tighten it with the pliers, again using the rag to prevent damage to the nut.

7 Double check that the nuts are snug and slowly turn on the valves to check for leaks.

8 Allow the water to run for a minute or so to make sure the task was successfully completed.

REPLACING A FAUCET CARTRIDGE OR A STEM

MATERIALS

Allen key (or a precision flathead screwdriver or a Phillips screwdriver), crescent wrench, and plumber's grease

1   Turn off the water valves under the sink for the hot and cold water. Double check that they're both off by running the faucet on hot and cold water. A little dribble might come out, but no constant flow should be streaming if it's completely shut off.

2   Make sure to close the sink stopper or cover the sink drain to ensure you don't lose any screws or pieces down the drain.

3   On the handle is a set screw that can be removed so you can get to the stem/cartridge. Sometimes, it's visible; other times, it's added under a piece of plastic. Remove that set screw to remove the handle from the stem/cartridge. (An Allen key or a precision flathead or Phillips screwdriver should get the job done).

4   You can remove the stem/cartridge in a variety of manners. Sometimes, it can be easily pulled out by hand; others might require a crescent wrench. Take your time with the removal.

5   Inspect the stem/cartridge to see how damaged the O-ring is. This can give you more of an idea of why this problem occurred. If the O-ring is completely broken or severely damaged, then chances are that age was the main villain of this story. And you might only need to replace that very inexpensive item and put everything back together. If it looks intact and not worn at all, then the stem/cartridge could just be faulty and needs to be replaced.

6   Brands and models of faucets will often require specific kinds of stems/cartridges, so make sure the one you have is compatible with your faucet. You can always take it to the hardware store and ask someone to help you match it to a new one to make sure you get the right part.

7   Once you have the compatible item in hand, then you can place the cartridge or stem. Be sure to use a little bit of plumber's grease on it so it's lubricated and ready to be slid into its "forever home." Think of it as a little bit like chub rub for your thighs. When you have your thighs rubbing against each other all day, it causes some problems! Plumber's grease is basically just chub rub for your metals.

8   Once your stem/cartridge is ready to go, slide it into the hole or twist it in nice and tight. You might need a crescent wrench to tighten up a nut to ensure it's snug.

9   Place the handle back on the cartridge/stem and screw in the set screw with the tool that previously helped you remove it.

10 Turn on the water valve slowly but all the way open.

11 Turn on the faucet to hot and cold water to see if the job was successfully completed.

If none of these worked for you, there might be a bigger problem that sadly this book isn't going to be able to guide you on. But none of that means you didn't learn something along the way or develop new skills you won't use down the road. I'm truly proud of you for taking on these tasks and doing so much. You're a rock star and you'll carry this knowledge into the next project.

CLEANING FAUCETS AND DRAINS

Now that you know how to repair and unclog drains, you'll want to know about smells and grime! Often, the previous procedures have already fixed these problems. Drains start to get smelly when clogs form, so by removing them, we might have already solved a big portion of this problem. However, the following are some extra tips that might help prevent further problems from developing.

TACKLING A SMELLY DRAIN

Pouring 1 gallon (3.8L) of boiling hot water with some dish soap down a drain once a month will go a long way toward preventing most clogs and, thus, smells—especially if the dish soap is one that's designed for oils and grease. You want enough soap to get a lather, usually about 1–2 spoonfuls.

For tougher problems, adding baking soda and vinegar might be even better. This method is often used as a clog remover, but in reality, it's best for preventative maintenance rather than a solution to a pre-existing problem.

Add 1 cup of baking soda and 2 cups of vinegar, then wait 15 minutes for it to fizz. This alone can do a great amount of cleaning for you. Then run hot water down the drain for about 1 minute to clear out any grime that might now be loosen up from the pour. Do this once a week while problems persist and then you can reduce the frequency over time and work toward doing this once a month.

REPLACING OR REPAIRING A SINK STOPPER

You might sometimes run across problems that you'll live with and allow those problems to continue because the inconvenience of learning how to confront them seems like more of a hurdle than the problem itself.

I feel that in the core of my heart—and I want to make space for that feeling and anxiety you might have attached to any task within this book. However, few repairs elicit that response within my own life quite like this one. This isn't a particularly hard repair, but it can be one that requires patience.

So let's tackle this one with nurturing care for ourselves and for the task at hand. Get your favorite snack and beverage to reward yourself once the repair is finished.

As with many of the repairs in this book, this one is subject to the make and the model of your sink. But on the whole, most stoppers function in a pretty similar way.

The stopper will have some type of hole on the bottom of it. That hole is where a metal rod goes through that's connected to your stopper lever. Once you push down, that lever puts downward pressure on the rod that applies upward pressure to the stopper.

Think of it like a seesaw: You're seated on one side of the seesaw with your feet on the ground and a friend is up in the air on the other side. If a third person came along and pushed down on your friend, you'd get lifted up as your friend touches the ground. This is the same effect for the stopper.

The stopper often gets free from its "seesaw" and just needs to be hooked back up. That's where you're going to start. If your stopper is cracked or damaged in any way, I'd suggest getting a new one that fits your previous one as closely as possible. You can get universal stoppers or an exact match at most hardware stores.

1   Go under the sink and place a pillow or something soft for you to rest your back on. This can be a tough and uncomfortable job, so be prepared for it if your sink requires being in a funky position.

2   Use your hand to unscrew the cap that holds the rod to the ball joint. Once the rod is out of way, you'll be able to place the stopper in the drain with the hole facing toward the rod. There will be a plastic gasket on the outside of the ball joint. Make sure to not lose that or you might have leaking issues later on.

3   Slide the back into the hole through the hole of the stopper—like thread going through the eye of the needle and often just as frustrating.

4   Screw the cap back on with the plastic gasket to make sure it's secure.

5   You can also adjust the stopper lever that's connected to the rod by lowering or raising the height where the two intersect. Raising it will make the stopper go higher and lowering it will make the stopper pop up less.

REMOVING AND REPAIRING TUB PLUGS

There are several main tub plug types and all of them have their own mechanism to remove them. I'm going to focus on the three most common plugs you'll see in most rentals. The others you might encounter will have various different removal methods. But use what you've learned so far in this book to help you troubleshoot issues you might face. I believe you'll do this, and with time and determination, you can pretty much accomplish anything.

MATERIALS

Phillips screwdriver

- **Lift and turn:** This stopper is installed by screwing a center set screw into the threaded center of the drain crossbar. The screw can be removed by going underneath the cap of the stopper. These are notorious for being difficult to remove if they're older, so keep trying and trust the process.

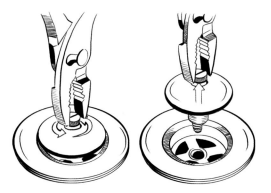

- **Push and pull:** This stopper is also attached to the drain with a set screw found under the cap of the stopper. Unscrew that and you'll be able to remove it.

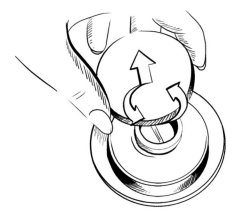

- **Trip lever:** This plug has two main separate pieces: a grate that covers the tub drain and a lever that's attached to the overflow drain. You can remove this plug by unscrewing the grate and then unscrewing the lever cover to the overflow drain. It'll then show a rod that's connected to the larger plug that stops up the tub. You can pull that up gently and remove it from the tub.

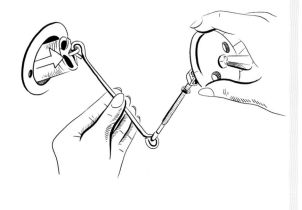

CAULKING

Messy jobs can be fun, but they often require an artistic eye. If a mess is created, that's okay! Focus on the art of it all. When applying caulk, you want it to blend in with nearby surfaces. If you can feather it and blend it with that intention, then you're doing an excellent job.

REMOVING CAULK

MATERIALS

utility knife or putty knife, rag, and denatured alcohol

1   Start by stripping the caulk. There are a few methods for doing this. You can use a utility knife or putty knife, slicing through the caulk and peeling it away. There are also specialized caulk removal tools designed to tear away caulk cleanly. Just be sure not to scratch the surface below the caulk with whatever tool you end up using.

2   Once the caulk has been removed, clean the area thoroughly of any residue left behind. Brush the area with a cloth dampened with denatured alcohol to prevent any damage to any surface you're working on or around. Let surfaces dry completely before beginning to apply any new caulk.

HOW TO APPLY CAULK

I recommend using a squeezable tube instead of a tube with a caulk gun—unless you plan on doing larger repairs. The control a handheld squeezable tube gives you is extremely beneficial, especially if you're not a pro at caulking.

squeezable silicone caulking and a spoon

1 Make sure the surface is clean and dry before applying the caulking. If this is in your bathroom, make sure to use silicone caulk that's mold- and mildew-resistant.

2 Applying caulking has just as much to do with how small and at what angle you cut the tip of the tube as anything else during the process. You want the size of the hole of your tube to be just a little more narrow than the total width you're aiming to cover. And cutting it at an angle will help direct the silicone toward the site rather than up in the air.

3 Place the nozzle up against the area you're caulking and smoothly drag it in the direction you desire. Make sure to hold it at a 45° angle in the direction you're going to help naturally smooth out some of the silicone as you go.

Handy Ma'am Tip:

If you're going in a straight line rather than a curve, I'd recommend placing painter's tape about ¼ inch (0.65cm) away from the desired area. Make sure to create a straight line all the way to the end of the area. This will help keep a straight line and will give a better overall finished look as well as keep the area cleaner. If the area is circular, this extra step might be unnecessary and harder to achieve.

4 Then you can either wet your finger and rub the caulk into the crease, feathering off the caulk, or you can use the back of a spoon to get a professional look. Either way you go, be sure to use consistent pressure in one direction as far as you can—ideally all the way to the end without any interruption.

5 When you're finished, know that you can always go over it again if you desire. Once you've got it looking to your satisfaction, remove the painter's tape if you applied it. Feather off the edge one last time to finish the job. And you did it! Remember, the purpose is to keep water out and to help seal things in. If it doesn't look perfect, as long as it does its job, then you did it wonderfully.

REPAIRING CAULKING THAT KEEPS CRACKING

If you've replaced your caulking, but it keeps cracking no matter how careful you are, you can try troubleshooting:

- Either something is moving or the surface didn't get clean and dry.
- Try again, being really careful to get the surface dry. You can wipe it with rubbing alcohol and let it dry to make sure all water has been removed.
- Don't use the shower or tub for 24 hours.
- Make sure the area around your tub isn't shifting or settling.
- If there's a bunch of air behind the caulk, it's going to crack. There should be no air pockets behind the caulk.
- You can add more caulk in there to have something behind it.
- Use your finger to push silicone into the air pocket while smoothing it out.
- Use foam filler to fill in behind the caulk.
- Use a foam backer rod (also known as caulk saver) behind the caulk for really large gaps.

Emotional Reset

Few rooms can stress us out like the bathroom—and everything in this chapter can cause you so much anxiety. We often overlook this room because we don't have parties there (HA-HA). It's a place where your guests don't spend much time or where they might not even go. So if you're the only one who's seeing it every day, then it can be easy for you to put it on the back burner and forget about it. But it's also one of the most functional spaces in your home. Everything in here serves a purpose, and when something's not functioning in a way that takes care of your needs, well, that can be hard.

So you owe it to yourself and your home to spend a little time now and again to make this space work for your needs. And you did a beautiful job. Getting professional results from these tasks isn't your desire. Getting the job done and making sure you feel good about it is your aim—and I think you're doing a pretty darn good job at that. And if it seems gross or messy, just remember, if you spend the time to do it now, you won't have to down the road. And that's very much a good thing.

7

TOILETS

THE BUBBLING GURGLING TOILET CLOG

Few areas in your home are used as much as the toilet and yet we give them so little attention. We certainly don't want to think about how they function—we just want them to do their job and leave us alone. However, like everything else, when your toilet is ignored and not cared for, larger issues and problems will arise. So get those gloves on, wear that nose plug, roll up those sleeves, and hang in there with me as we talk about all things toilets!

Handy Ma'am Tip:

Remember to check your water shut-off valves at the toilet before any emergency happens. This can save yourself a lot of headaches in the future!

PLUNGER-FREE FIXES

If your toilet is overflowing because of a clog, you're in need of an immediate remedy. Having the right supplies is definitely going to help, but sometimes we don't have a plunger on hand when these things go awry.

MATERIALS

bowl, dish soap, and 1 gallon (3.8L) of water

1 Go under the toilet and turn off the shutoff valves. This will prevent the water from further entering your tank and causing a flooding accident in your home.

2 Pour 3 cups of the dish soap and ½ gallon (1.9L) of hot water, but make sure it's not boiling, which can cause your toilet to crack.

3 Pour the soapy water into the toilet bowl at a steady pace—be sure not to dump it in all at once. Wait 2 minutes and pour in another ½ gallon (1.9L) of hot water.

4 Turn the water back on and flush the toilet after 1 minute.

In most cases, the dish soap will act as a lubricant for the blockage and help release it without the use of a plunger or auger. This is the cleanest method for releasing a toilet clog.

Handy Ma'am Tip:

Do NOT use boiling hot water!

- The extreme heat can crack the porcelain toilet.

- The extreme heat can also melt the wax ring and cause future leaks from under the base of your toilet.

Other creative options are:

- You can use a scrub brush by filling the bowl with water and pushing the brush into the drain and working it back and forth. This works because it's applying air pressure to the drain and pushing the water around. This often has to be done quickly and forcefully to make sure the toilet doesn't overflow on you.

- You can also add a plastic bag around a scrub brush to help create even more pressure. Make sure to tie a very tight knot around the brush so you don't lose the plastic bag in the toilet. Having a bucket on the side you can place the scrub brush in after you're done will go a long way toward preventing a larger mess in your bathroom.

THE PLUNGER METHOD

If none of the previous methods solve the problem, the next option is to use a plunger or toilet auger.

The first thing to determine when plunging a toilet is what kind of plunger you'll need. The most common plunger we think of is called a cup plunger. This isn't a toilet plunger! In fact, it's designed for sink and tubs, not for a toilet. A cup plunger won't give a great seal in the drain, which is the most important consideration when dealing with this kind of clog.

- A toilet with a rounded drain hole is going to be best paired with a **flange plunger.** The flange plunger has a top hat design. This "hat" feature can be flared out or pushed inward. For best results, having this feature flared out will help make a perfect seal.

- A toilet with an elongated drain hole is best paired with a **beehive plunger.** A flange plunger can work fine with this but doesn't make as tight of a seal as the beehive does.

- The **bellows plungers,** commonly known as the accordion plunger, is difficult to create a seal because of its being made out of plastic rather than rubber. But it's by far the superior plunger for tough clogs and is absolutely my favorite kind. The pleated sides help push the water into the drain as you're pumping the plunger and the shear force releases most clogs from the toilet.

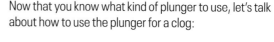

Handy Ma'am Tip:

When it comes to cleaning your plungers, I do NOT recommend using bleach. Bleach can destroy the elasticity of the rubber or crack it. The best way to clean it is with hot, soapy water with your favorite disinfectant. Let it sit in a 5-gallon (19L) pail if you have one and then scrub the plunger and put it back in place for next time.

Now that you know what kind of plunger to use, let's talk about how to use the plunger for a clog:

1 To make sure you're not causing an overflow once you put the plunger into the toilet, slowly lower the plunger and pour in ½ gallon (1.9L) of water. Not only does air help dislodge a clog, but so will water and the force of that water.

2 Angle the plunger at a 35–45° angle into the drain. Make sure there's a nice, strong seal all around the plunger as best as you can do.

3 Start to slowly plunge the plunger into the drain. After a few pumps, vigorously start pumping harder.

4 It can take a few seconds or a few minutes for the plunging to fully release a clog. If it doesn't release right away, don't get discouraged. Hang in there and keep trying. After the fourth or fifth time, if it doesn't release, then move on to the next step, which is a toilet auger.

THE AUGER METHOD

If a plunger didn't release the clog, it's time to use a toilet auger. Toilet augers are much heavier duty compared with toilet plungers. I never recommend getting the cheapest toilet auger. I always recommend getting the ones that are between $40–65. These tend to be thicker and larger, which means they'll fit the entire inside of the drain of the toilet.

Often, the culprit in these scenarios is a backup or clog inside the S-trap in your toilet. The S-trap is designed to prevent something called backflow. Backflow is the smell and all that disgusting stuff that can hide inside your toilet and the drain itself. This is why sometimes you might be repeating the declogging processes you learned earlier every couple of weeks.

MATERIALS

handheld auger (I prefer the Cobra Skinny Drain Snake)

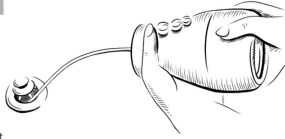

1   Make sure to get a toilet auger that extends to about 10 feet (3m) long and has a bulbed tip.

2   Slowly feed the wire into the drain, being careful to not accidentally rub the metal up against the porcelain to avoid damage. Make sure to feed the auger at an angle.

3   The auger will have a handle that can be rotated like a clock. You can push up and down on the auger to help guide the wire down the drain, but as you're pushing it up and down, turn it clockwise. That motion as it cycles through the toilet will scrape inside all the way down to the bottom of the toilet. This will get every bit of debris and everything that could be forming inside your toilet.

4   Repeat this process two to three times, and if the blockage isn't fully released, then the clog might be farther down the drain. At this point, I recommend putting in a maintenance request.

Cleaning a toilet auger can be a little bit more of a task and the one I recommend uses bleach and hot water. As you're pulling the auger out of the toilet, rub down each part with a paper towel or disposable rag. You want to prevent rusting as well as problems down the road, so getting as much of that water soaked up as possible is ideal. Many toilet augers will come with a bag you can store it in. I recommend getting a canvas bag for it if one isn't provided.

MYSTERIOUS, MISCELLANEOUS TOILET PROBLEMS

REPAIRING A LOOSE TOILET SEAT

There is nothing more frustrating than a loose toilet seat, but there are a few things you can do to try to prevent this from reoccurring.

MATERIALS

flathead screwdriver, Phillips screwdriver, and silicone caulking

1   Up by the base of the toilet seat should be a cover that can be opened up with a flathead screwdriver to reveal a nylon screw.

2   The nylon screw will have a nut underneath the toilet that has flanges on the side, so you don't even have to hold that nut in place when you're screwing in the screw. Use a Phillips screwdriver to screw it in a little bit tighter.

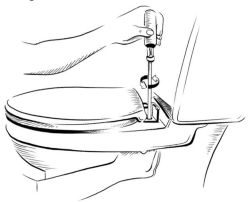

3   If that doesn't solve the problem, then move on to applying adhesive. Try a more temporary option, such as silicone caulking, first.

4   Use the Phillips screwdriver to remove the screw, making sure to grab the nut so it doesn't fall on the floor and get lost.

5   Put a little silicone caulk on the threads of the screw.

6   Give it a little bit of time before you tighten it in there—let it gel up a bit first.

7   Put the screw back in place, place the nut underneath, and begin tightening the screw.

8   The caulk will adhere to the nylon nut underneath and will hopefully give you more hold.

For a more permanent solution you can use Loctite plastic bond or any type of adhesive that's designed for plastics and nylon. Be sure you use adhesive not designed for metals because it won't have the right amount of bond you'll need for this job.

The last option is replacing the toilet seat altogether. There are so many brands and models of toilet seats that are designed to never loosen up and are still easily removable. Most of them range between $22–$35. The seat is something you can replace during your rental period and then swap in the old one before you move out. Just note which type of toilet you have: standard or elongated.

Handy Ma'am Tip:

Some older homes will have metal bolts that may be rusted and difficult to remove. You may need a socket wrench, screw driver, or WD-40 to get it loose.

REPLACING OR TIGHTENING A TOILET HANDLE

Toilets will vary in design and model, and this also extends to toilet handles. But universally, a toilet handle will have some type of nut—either metal or plastic—that's in the toilet tank itself.

You can take the toilet lid off, take a look, and see what's happening. It can be:

- This handle is indeed broken.
- The nut is missing.
- The handle isn't tightened up against the porcelain.

MATERIALS

adjustable pliers

1   The solution is often simple and you can just hold the toilet handle on the outside and then put your hand in the toilet tank and tighten the nut. Or you can use adjustable pliers to get a firmer grip and tighten it up.

2   If this doesn't work or the problem happens again, then you'll have to replace the handle altogether. To do that, remove the nut with adjustable pliers, then slide the handle out.

3   The handle will connect to the flapper. It's often a hook, wire, or another mechanism that pulls it up to get the job done. Whatever it is, make sure to disconnect it before you take it out.

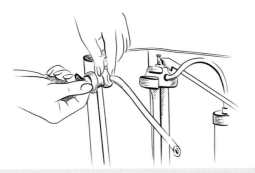

Handy Ma'am Tip:

If you don't want to work with a toilet tank filled with water, then you can close the water valve down below the tank and then flush the toilet. That will release all the water in the tank without bringing more in so you don't have to work with toilet water in the tank (although the water in the toilet is clean).

4   Take the handle to the hardware store to find a match.

5   Insert the handle throughout the slot, reattach it to the flapper, and place and tighten the nut on the back until the handle is firmly in place.

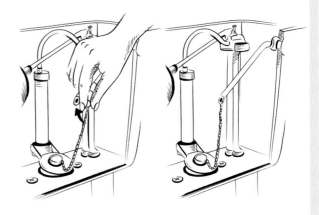

6   Test the handle to make sure it works properly.

FIXING A CONSTANTLY RUNNING TOILET

A toilet that keeps on running can be solved with one very simple fix—and that's the flapper. On most toilets, the flapper is a rubber gasket that sits over the drain that goes into the toilet bowl. This is controlled by the toilet handle.

Over time, that flapper can go bad: It can crack, dry out, or have calcium buildup from hard water. These issues can cause a whole bunch of different problems for that flapper. You can take a look at the flapper and see how aged it is. If it's pretty beat up, the chances are just replacing it might be the best option. But if it just looks dirty, then cleaning it can also work well.

MATERIALS

dish soap, rag, and adjustable pliers

1   Make sure to empty the tank by turning off the water valve down below the toilet and then flushing the toilet.

2   Using regular dish soap and hot water with a nice rag can do a pretty good job of cleaning the flapper.

3   If you need to, you can disconnect the handle from the flapper to take it out and clean it better or replace it. There are different ways to disconnect it, but one of the most common ways is to remove the little hook from the eyehole it's attached to.

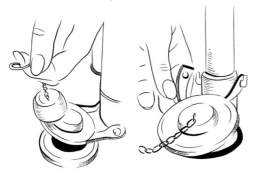

Handy Ma'am Tip:

Your flapper may just have some calcium or lime buildup on it, or in the hole that it closes on. Drain the tank and then use a plastic knife, a green Brillo sponge, or another scraper to remove the buildup occasionally. You'll know this is the issue if your toilet randomly starts to fill up even when it wasn't recently flushed.

4   If it doesn't have that, it might have some type of link, like a piece of string or even some connecting wire, that could also be disconnected.

5   Once you have the flapper removed from the chain it's attached to, there are typically two slots that are on the side of the flapper you can then also disconnect to fully remove the flapper.

6   If you do need to replace the flapper, take it to a hardware store and try to find the best match possible. You're not always going to get an exact match—some are universal—but the best thing you can do is make a pretty close match and then attach the new flapper to the wire or whatever mechanism the toilet has—and hopefully that solves the problem. If it doesn't solve the problem of a constantly running tank, then replacing the fill valve (page 95) will be the best solution.

INSTALLING A BIDET

Installing a bidet can be a game-changer for those who care about having a very clean butt—like me!

There are two main types of different bidets: hot water and cold water. In most places in the United States, a cold water bidet is just fine. The water's not going to get too much below 60°F (16°C) and it's going to feel comfortable when used. Typically, it's going to rest somewhere between 54–58°F (12–14°C), but it all depends on what region you're in and what kind of pressure you might have in your water.

There are parts of the United States and all over the world that might have colder water. If that's something you're concerned about, then I do recommend getting yourself a hot water bidet if you're able to. The major difference between a cold water bidet and a hot water bidet—other than the temperature itself—is how the water's brought in. Both bidets take water from the supply line that goes to the tank, but the hot water bidet will also need a hot water source. This source comes from the hot water line under your sink, so you'll need to make sure the toilet is next to your sink to be able to attach a hot water bidet.

To install a **cold water bidet:**

MATERIALS

adjustable pliers, wrench, and a Phillips screwdriver

1   Turn off the shut-off valve underneath the toilet tank. Then flush the toilet to drain the water out of the tank and ensure it's not running.

2   Disconnect the supply line to the toilet and insert the adapter for the bidet. The bidet typically comes with an adapter that will have two threaded rods and internal threads on the top.

3   The supply line should go to the bottom thread of the adapter. Lead the supply line from the bidet to the adapter, tightening it with a wrench.

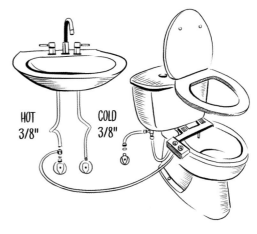

4   Once the supply line is attached to the bidet, you can remove the toilet seat by taking the nylon screws out, putting the bidet on the surface of the toilet, returning the toilet seat, threading the rods through the toilet seat and the bidet, and tightening the nuts down below.

5   You can now slowly turn the water valve back on from underneath the toilet. Make sure you open up the water valve all the up and take your time—there's no rush here. Then you can turn on the bidet, but when you do so, make sure you understand that the bidet might shoot at you. So putting something there that will block the spray but still allow you to test the bidet would be ideal.

If you do want to install a hot water bidet, there are some extra steps.

To install a **hot water bidet:**

adjustable pliers, wrench, and a Phillips screwdriver

Handy Ma'am Tip:

Some companies will give you threaded tape and some won't. If a company doesn't supply you with threaded tape, don't add it yourself. Adding threaded tape or plumber's tape to products that don't recommend it can cause leaking and cracking.

1 Typically, a hot water bidet comes with one long white tube or another color tube. This tube goes right into the major component of the bidet itself, where the supply line is going and where you can turn all the knobs and everything. This tube will fit right into its little slot. It usually says hot water on it so you know which one it is.

2 You can run it behind the toilet or run it to the side depending on where your sink is. Some people will have faucets that don't have any cabinetry and just a bare sink with an open area underneath it—and that's perfect for a bidet. But if you have a cabinet, you'll have to drill a hole to run the bidet through there. If that's not something you want to do, you should keep that in mind when choosing which kind of bidet to install.

3 Once you get the tube where you need it to be directly under the water valve, turn off the water valve.

4 Disconnect the supply line, add the adapter, reconnect the supply line to the top of the adapter, and then insert the tube right into the adapter.

5 Slowly open the water valve, and as you're doing that, check for possible leaks everywhere—just triple check if you can to put your mind at ease and then you can open up the water all the way before checking that the bidet works. And then you're good to go!

Remember, old bidets are going to be installed a little bit differently and this might not be the way your bidet should be installed, but this gives you a general idea of how its done, with maybe a tip or trick or two that can help you along the way.

FIXING A WHISTLING OR OVERFLOWING TANK

There are few things as annoying as a whistling toilet. It can pulsate into your eardrums and cause you so much stress. But a whistling toilet is often caused by one specific thing—and that's your fill valve.

Your fill valve is what brings all the water into your toilet. It's inside your toilet tank and works in tandem with the toilet flapper. The fill valve will have a device on it called a float. The float will go down when water is released into the bowl, and the farther the float goes down, the more water will be brought in from the supply line to get it back up to level.

Over time, the more and more water this fill valve takes in, the more worn out it will get. It can also get damaged from calcium or mineral buildup from hard water. That might cause your fill valve to begin doing things like whistling or overflowing. While parts of the fill valve can go bad, it's not possible to replace these pieces individually, so it's best to replace the whole fill valve as one piece. A fill valve can be easily replaced.

Note: This fix will work with the majority of toilets, though there are a wide variety of toilets out there and yours may be different.

MATERIALS

adjustable pliers, wrench, and a Phillips screwdriver

1 Turn off the water valve to the toilet—underneath the toilet—and then flush the toilet to empty the tank.

2 Remove the lid and float ball.

3 Place a bucket on the floor underneath the supply line to catch excess water when you disconnect the supply line.

4 Use adjustable pliers to disconnect the larger nut that's holding the fill valve in place.

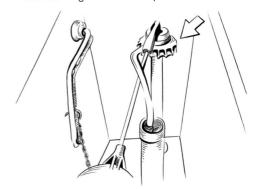

5 Remove the fill valve and clean the area so it's free of any dirt or mineral buildup.

6 You might need to adjust the new fill valve prior to putting it in place. Refer to the instructions for installation of the fill valve.

7 Insert the valve into the opening and use the pliers to tighten the nut from below.

8 Put the refill tube into the overflow pipe and reattach the float ball.

9 Reconnect the supply line.

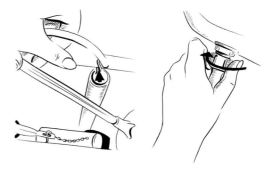

10 Turn on the water slowly, check for leaks, and check the water level.

I always advise people to splurge on a very good fill valve. The better quality will last longer and be more durable for the duration of your time in the home.

Emotional Reset

We often look at a toilet and think of how gross and disgusting it is—and we don't want to go near it. But as I demonstrated by laying out everything in this section, a lot of this is fairly straightforward and it's okay if you experience a hurdle or two that make you feel like this was more difficult than what I might be making it out to be. It's okay you're at that point. But there's an almost demystifying part of this section. Toilets can be expensive, but the components in the toilet—from the flapper and the fill valve to the flush valve, the handle, and even bidets—are relatively inexpensive. What's really expensive is just making sure we don't damage the porcelain toilet itself, but everything else is accessible and can be accomplished. All you need is patience, the proper protective equipment, and to make sure you're staying clean and away from all that disgusting grime and natural blockage that you might encounter.

But ultimately, remember this: You can do this. Nothing in this section needs to be done by a professional, but if you do get to that point and you don't think you're able to do something, that's okay. It doesn't make you lesser, doesn't make you bad at this. It just means this situation you're encountering right now is a little bit tougher than where you are at right now—and that's okay because the next time you encounter it might be the time you can solve it yourself. But you'll never know if you don't allow yourself to take on that task. So I'm proud of you for trying and I'm proud of you for reading this section. You're doing a great job.

SHOWERS

SO FRESH AND SO CLEAN

Showers are one of the most personal things for me. It's where I do a lot of thinking and feel the most me, and I like my showers to make me feel comfortable and safe. A properly functioning showerhead can often help with that goal. If the shower is also your safe space, then you know having the right water pressure and settings can dramatically improve your showering experience. You don't need all the bells and whistles, but the showerheads you find in an apartment sometimes don't meet all your needs. If you find a showerhead that works best for you, here's how you can install it and make your shower time more personal.

REPLACING A SHOWERHEAD

Before you begin installing a showerhead, if you notice a red substance around where the showerhead attaches, that might be red Loctite, which is nearly impossible to remove. Make sure to talk to your landlord for help and don't try to remove it yourself.

MATERIALS

new showerhead, threaded tape (Teflon tape), rag, and adjustable pliers

1 Place the rag on the old showerhead to protect it from damage and to add grip to prevent the pliers from slipping.

2 Twist the pliers lefty loosey and then use your hand to unscrew the showerhead the rest of the way.

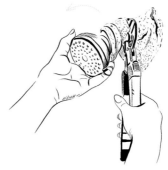

3 Peel off the old thread tape and use the rag to clean and wipe away any debris on threads of the pipe.

4 Wrap a new piece of thread tape around the threads of the pipe (no more than three times). Some newer showerheads don't require thread tape and it's best not to use it if the packaging says not to.

5 Make sure the rubber gasket or washer is inside the showerhead before placing the showerhead on the pipe.

6 Use your hand to twist the showerhead onto the pipe.

7 Use the rag and the pliers to snugly tighten the showerhead on the pipe. Go slowly and be sure not to overtighten. Otherwise, you can damage the showerhead.

FIXING A WHISTLING SHOWERHEAD

A whistling sound coming from your showerhead is often caused by a water regulator washer in a new showerhead. The washer is meant to regulate the amount of water being used, but it can flip sideways inside the showerhead or get worn out from hard water. When either or both of these things happen, your showerhead can become a noisy menace. You can fix this by removing the regulator altogether. It won't affect the performance of the showerhead. If anything, the showerhead's efficiency will only improve.

MATERIALS

rag, adjustable pliers, and a flathead screwdriver

1 Place a rag on the showerhead and twist lefty loosey with the pliers.

2 Use your hand to unscrew the showerhead the rest of the way.

3 Use a flathead screwdriver or something nice and sharp to carefully remove the regulator.

4 Use the rag and pliers to snugly tighten the showerhead on the pipe. Go slowly and be sure not to overtighten. Otherwise, you can damage the showerhead.

FIXING A LOOSE SHOWER HANDLE

We all know how annoying loose handles are. Constant use can loosen the set screw of the handle, so it might need to be tightened up from time to time. Some handles with a visible set screw can be tightened with an Allen key, but others are hiding in plain sight. There's often a plastic cover that rests in the center of the handle, which can be pried open with the point of a sharp knife. Poke out the cover and then tighten the screw with a screwdriver (most commonly a Phillips screwdriver). If the screw keeps loosening, you can use a little silicone caulk on the threads to help it stay. This will be enough to hold it but not enough to make it a nightmare to remove later.

FIXING A WHISTLING SHOWER FAUCET (SPOUT) OR TUB DIVERTER

Often when a spout is starting to wear down, the diverter lever can go bad. This can be caused by the gasket wearing out or the plastic cracking inside the spout itself. A whistling noise can occur when the shower is on and often the spout will still produce water below while the shower is on. This means the diverter isn't going all the way up to block the flow of water when it should all be going up to your shower.

MATERIALS

utility knife, rag, Allen key or flathead screwdriver, and silicone caulking

1   If there's caulking around the spout, use the sharp point of the utility knife to remove it.

2   Make sure the water is all the way off on the water spout and cover the drain with the rag so you don't lose screws or parts during the process.

3   You can remove the spout two ways: with a set screw underneath the spout (often an Allen key) or by angling a long flathead screwdriver inside the spout opening and twisting the spout lefty loosey. This will reveal the actual drain spout.

4   Slide on the new tub spout and either screw in the set screw or use your hand to twist on the spout.

5   Seal the area around the new spout with silicone caulking.

Emotional Reset

Plumbing is often seen as a very hard, specialized task, but all the projects listed in this section are actually pretty straightforward. Your skill level is going to dictate if you're able to approach a lot of these, but all the ones I've mentioned require a few tools. A screwdriver, adjustable pliers, and a sharp utility knife are often the only ones you need. A trusty rag also goes a long way!

It's important to understand that the limitations you put on yourself for various things—from electrical to plumbing—are because you don't want to mess up and have a large flood or cause a bigger problem than you started with. All that's absolutely notable and worth some extra caution, but there are also things like showerheads, door handles, tub diverters, and spouts that can be fixed with just a little bit of know-how, a little bit of patience, and a lot a lot of trust in yourself.

I hope laying this out for you and showing you how approachable these can be can lead to your learning other things. Many times, the things that need fixing in your apartment or home can be solved with a little bit more investigation. If you have confidence in yourself and you want to continue learning, I always encourage watching videos online and allowing yourself to learn along the way. That's how I've learned—and that's how many professionals learn too. Sometimes, all you need is to see this is approachable for you and to give yourself the green light to give it a try. I hope this chapter gives you the green light—and I hope you have fun on this journey!

WALL REPAIR, PAINTING, AND MOUNTING

FINDING THE MYTHICAL WALL STUD

Finding an object hidden behind a fully enclosed wall is difficult. Don't let others mock you for not knowing how to find a stud or say you must use a stud finder. While that's a great tool, it can be cost-prohibitive and learning to use one correctly can take time. Instead, you can use this simple little method that will help you not only find a wall stud but also get you all kinds of attention at the next party you attend.

Words to Know:

Studs are vertical pieces of sturdy material used to support the frame of your home. It's important to hang heavy items, like TVs, shelves, or heavy mirrors, on a stud because it can support the weight of the object far better than weaker materials, like drywall. Some houses are built with fancy metal studs, but most rentals just use thick wood and nails or screws. In this case, you'll use a magnet to find the metal fasteners and locate the stud.

THE MAGNET METHOD PROCESS

MATERIALS

paper towel, magnet, metal chain/necklace

You'll need to get a magnet from a hardware store or a craft store if you don't have one on hand. The kind that comes in a pack of 6–10 for under $3 will work nicely for this. Larger magnets that cover more surface area will save you some time.

Don't just look at the section of the wall where you're holding the magnet. If the magnet sticks to an area directly above an outlet or it stays stuck as you move it up and down vertically, you don't want to drill there. You've likely found a pipe or electrical housing.

1. Place a piece of paper towel on the wall and then the magnet on top of the paper towel. (This will protect the surface from getting scuffed up.)

2. Place a metal chain or necklace on the magnet.

3. Move the magnet across the wall, right to left, in a wide sweeping motion. You'll feel a tug. To make sure this is a screw or nail head, slide the magnet up and down. If it loses its pull quickly, then it's a stud rather than a pipe.

4. Leave the magnet and chain on the wall. You can drill into the stud directly under where the chain is located or right above the magnet.

5. You'll know if it worked by wiggling the screw. If you can wiggle it out, the process didn't work. Give it another try to find the stud until the screw is firmly in place in the stud.

MERCURY AND THE MANY PATCHES

Everyone has various holes that need patching on their walls. The type of patch needed all depends on what size hole you're dealing with. Drywall repair is a beast and likely something you'd automatically think of hiring a professional for. But I'm here to tell you otherwise—I know you can do this.

When I first started doing drywall 15 years ago, I was atrocious at it. I had no skill set whatsoever. And even then, there were some patches I did that I'm still very proud of today because all it takes is patience and trying until you get it right. The best part about doing drywall is that if you don't get it right the first time, you can try and try again. Don't rush the steps and keep going until you're comfortable with it.

First and foremost, having the right supplies all depends on what size hole you're working on, so start there.

SPACKLE VS. JOINT COMPOUND

Spackle is a lightweight material that doesn't do well long term. If you have a larger patch to cover, I wouldn't recommend using spackle because it's not going to adhere, be strong enough, or do the job you really need it to do. It also can be harder to blend it into the wall.

You also might be tempted to use toothpaste and other quick fixes you've seen on the internet for patching up small holes, but I'm going to encourage you to not do that. Chances are that while these hacks might not cause a problem in a structural sense, they'll never look great cosmetically. Save the technician, save the new renter, save the person who might be inhabiting this home later on in life the headaches and do it right the first time.

Joint compound is what's used when first installing drywall. So when you're using it to patch a hole, you're using what's already on the wall itself—and that's why I like it. It's also very affordable. I recommend getting at least 1 quart (¼ gallon [0.95L]). Once you open the container, the shelf life is 6–8 months.

PATCHING SMALL HOLES

If you're talking about pinhole patches, like nail holes or holes that are just under the diameter of a pen, then spackle can be used for a hole like this with an all-in-one applicator. All-in-one applicators can be purchased from several different companies, but the one I prefer is from 3M.

MATERIALS

scraper, spackle, and an all-in-one applicator (with a sanding pad)

1 Use a scraper to apply a small amount of spackle to the area.

2 Use the back of the applicator to press the spackle into the hole, scrape off any excess, and smooth the spackle down around the edges.

3 Let it dry for 10–15 minutes.

4 Use the sander on the top of the applicator to sand around the hole in a circular motion. You can lightly go over it once or twice, but you don't want to go over it too much.

Handy Ma'am Tip:

If the area has texture and you're afraid of the new spackle not being texturized, you can actually use the spackle as a way to add a little bit of texture. Add the spackle, and while it's still wet, tap a textured sponge on the spackle. It might not be perfect, but it can add enough texture in small little areas to do the trick.

PATCHING MEDIUM HOLES

If you have larger holes—up to roughly the size of a bottle cap or 1 inch (2.5cm)—they can be fixed with just joint compound. For holes between 1-6 inches (2.5-15cm), use the California patch method on page 110.

MATERIALS

joint compound, putty knife or 4-6-inch (10-15cm) joint knife, an affordable mud pan, and drywall tape or fiber tape (also known as mesh tape)

1   Cut the drywall tape slightly larger than the hole, with enough clearance to create a good grip.

2   Cover the hole with the tape.

3   Use the mud pan to combine the joint compound with water until it resembles the consistency of pancake batter.

4   Use a putty knife to cover the area with the mud. Use a nice, smooth movement, as if you're waving in one straight motion.

5   Fill the area entirely. If it's a small hole, don't be afraid to apply compound to the wall 2 inches (5cm) around the hole.

Handy Ma'am Tip:

Even if it's a small hole, you're going to want to make sure you cover more than what you actually see to create the illusion of flatness. When you're talking about drywall repair, you're not talking about making it flat—you're not going to be able to do that. There will always be a slight variation, but what you're doing is creating the illusion of flatness. So building an "on ramp" into it and away from it will be ideal. And the longer the ramp and taller the ramp, the less you're going to see it. Some holes won't need this; others will. It all depends on what you're encountering.

There's a little bit of artistry that goes into this, so if you're someone who's great with a paintbrush and understands how to shade and how to work with light, you're going to do wonders with mud. And if you don't get it right the first time, that's okay. Keep trying. I have zero artistic ability when it comes to painting or anything of that sort, but I think I'm a wonderful mudder. And if I had just a little bit more artistic flare, I bet you I'd be a legend.

MAKING A CALIFORNIA PATCH

If you're talking about holes wider than 1-6 inches (2.5-15cm), you'll want to replace them with drywall. My preferred method is a product called Presto Patch from DAP. It's basically an instant California patch.

A California patch is one of many different ways to cover a hole in drywall, but essentially what you're doing is keeping a piece of drywall intact and putting cardboard all around it. Drywall is just plaster with two pieces of cardboard on either side. Think of drywall like a plaster sandwich.

The Presto Patch is easy because it comes with a template, but you can easily create your own.

1   Cut a piece of drywall to at least 2 inches (5cm) bigger on each side than the hole.

2   Turn it over so you see the brown backing and measure 1 inch (2.5cm) from the edge. Draw a line 1 inch (2.5cm) in on each side.

3   Use a utility knife to cut into the back of the drywall—but not all the way through—so the paper on the front is still intact.

4   Break off the back side and plaster of the drywall, leaving the paper on the front of the drywall intact. This will allow you to put the drywall into the hole and use the paper to adhere it to the wall.

5   Now that you have your patch, place it on the wall and trace it without including the extra paper around the outside. You just want to trace the interior portion of the patch.

6   Use a drywall knife to cut around the hole in the wall so it's the same size as your piece of drywall (not the entire patch). Cut it on an angle if you can to bevel the edges and allow for better adhesion of the joint compound.

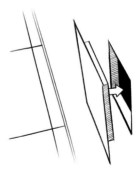

7   Once you have the drywall around the hole removed, you're ready to mud and insert the patch. Add some joint compound to your mud pan and add enough water to reach a pancake-like consistency.

8   Add the joint compound to the surface around the hole first, then apply the patch and add more joint compound on top of that.

9   If the compound isn't wet enough when you put the patch on, it will bubble up and create problems later on. When you're applying the joint compound, it's okay if it's a messy job. What matters is what it looks like when all is said and done, so take your time.

14 It's always best to sand in the same direction. If you go up and down, you're way more likely to scrape the wall. But if you're going down, picking it up, and then going down again, it's going to make it look much smoother when it's all said and done.

15 Once you're all done, then you're on to the paint job. See pages 114–115 for the priming and painting process.

Handy Ma'am Tip:

If you're afraid about all the dust getting in the air when you're sanding, you can wet the sanding block regularly while you're using it. This does make the process take a lot longer, but it does a very effective job at keeping the dust minimal.

Handy Ma'am Tip:

This compound application technique takes some time and it's all about pressure and where you put your fingers on the blade. If you want to use a larger knife, a 14-inch (36cm) blade is ideal, but if you don't have that in your budget, you can absolutely use a joint knife for this job. You might have a little bit more sanding to do, but that's all right.

- At the end, always err on the side of getting it as smooth as possible. Then you can sand all around it and do your best to feather in the ramps. Clean up any messy spots with a wet rag.

10 Add a good bit of mud to the joint knife. Starting in the middle, do one big scrape down through the center of the patch and then go across the sides.

11 Press on the outside of the joint knife and go down one side. On the other side, press outward on the joint knife and go down so the blade is pressed away from the center rather than in the middle. What you're doing is making a runway—a nice long ramp in the center. You want to build ramps all around the center of the patch. Adding the joint compound might take you to two to three coats to get the look you want, but don't sand in between the coats— allow it to just exist the way it is.

12 If you're still not sure if you got the patch smooth enough, take your joint knife or a longer mud blade and place the edge of it on the wall where you'ved patched and mudded. Look for gaps between the blade and the wall.

13 If you got it all filled in smoothly and feathered off on all the sides, the next step is sanding. Using a 360-grit sanding block should be good enough, but can also use a 120-grit or 200-grit sanding block. My favorite sanding blocks are the ones that can easily fit in your hand for gripping.

PATCHING LARGE HOLES

When you have holes in your walls that are wider than 6 inches (15cm), you'll need a bit more than a Presto Patch or a California patch. You'll also need a bit more durability to keep your drywall stable and secure. You're going to do what's called the support board patch.

You'll need some scrap wood for this. You'll want two to four even cuts. In an ideal world, they'd be similar in size. This patch is using scrap wood behind the drywall to support the drywall patch you'll be placing on the wall. The larger the hole is, the larger your scraps of wood should be and the more scraps of wood you'll need. A 6-inch (15cm) hole might only need one to two small scraps of wood, while a 12-inch (30.5cm) hole might need four to six scraps of wood. Do what you think is best for your circumstances!

MATERIALS

drywall, 2-4 scraps of wood, utility knife, drywall knife, joint knife, joint compound, drywall tape, screws, Phillips screwdriver, mud pan, 360-grit sanding block, and a pencil

1 Cut the drywall patch slightly larger than the hole. Place that over the hole and use a pencil to outline that patch on the wall.

2 Use this template to cut the hole with a drywall knife so the hole is the same size as the patch. Go slowly, taking off small pieces at a time so you can look out for wires, conduit, or anything else behind the wall.

3 Screw the scrap wood into the drywall, with half the wood behind the existing wall and the other half showing in the hole. The drywall patch will screw into the scrap wood, so you want to see the scrap wood in the hole when you're done attaching the pieces to the existing wall.

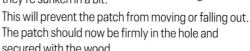

4 Screw two screws into the wall to attach the scrap wood so it can't move. Make sure the screw recesses into the wall so you can cover it with joint compound when you're done.

5 Continue to attach the scrap wood to the outer edges of the hole until you have enough for your drywall patch to adhere to, usually two to four pieces. If you use two pieces, make sure they're on opposite sides of the hole for stability.

6 Place the drywall patch snugly into the hole and screw in two screws through the patch and into each piece of scrap wood behind it, making sure to recess the screws so they're sunken in a bit. This will prevent the patch from moving or falling out. The patch should now be firmly in the hole and secured with the wood.

7 Outline the patch with drywall tape, being careful not to overlap the tape pieces because this will cause it to get too bulky in that area.

8 Apply the joint compound (see page 111), making sure to fill in the gaps and cover the drywall tape well.

9 Once all the coats are done and dry, sand the dried compound. (See page 111).

THE FUN-DAMENTALS OF PAINTING

Painting and priming are things a lot of people think they can do pretty simply and easily, but the processes can be a little tricky.

Priming is essential to any painting job. Skipping priming can lead to sticky walls, bits of original color popping through, and extra top coats. Ultimately, this will cost you more money and much more effort.

MATCHING PAINT

Matching paint colors can be done in multiple ways. If you have a quarter-sized piece of paint that's ripping off the wall, you can remove it, take it to almost any hardware store or paint store, and they'll match that paint.

Alternatively, you can go to a hardware store and get color sample cards to test at home. This is a great way to do it and make it more cost-effective because the exact paint match will often cost a lot more money. Paint stores will often charge you for a match made using their computers and technology and then $50 or more for the gallon of paint itself. But the paint cards are free and can typically get you within margins.

If you're just doing little patch jobs, sometimes you can ask maintenance at your apartment if it's okay for you to get some of the leftover paint that was used in the apartment for touchup jobs. Some people are going to be okay with this. Some technicians will absolutely hate this. Some will charge you and some won't. As a fellow maintenance technician, I never had a problem giving that paint to tenants. I trusted they were doing the best they could and I also know that lived-in apartments are always going to have some dings.

CHOOSING A FINISH

There are several different glosses and types of paint you can choose from. The following are in order from matte to shiny:

- Flat
- Matte
- Eggshell enamel
- Satin enamel
- Semi gloss enamel
- High gloss enamel

Knowing which one to use is often a struggle for people. Nine times out of 10, I'd say stay away from flat paint. Flat is great for little odd jobs here and there, but for your walls, I don't recommend it. Typically, what you'll get for most of your walls is eggshell or satin. Eggshell has a little bit less of a gloss, whereas satin has just a tiny bit more. Semi-gloss and high gloss are way more common in kitchens and bathrooms because they help your walls be easily cleaned. The more sheen walls have, the better and more effectively they can be cleaned later.

PAINTING A SMALL PATCH

If you just have a tiny hole you're trying to cover up with paint or you're trying to cover a small patch, you can just paint that area a little bit above and a little bit below.

Here's a very effective technique for painting a small patch:

Paint and 2-inch (5cm) straight paint brush

1   Put just a little bit of paint on the paint brush—seriously, only use a tiny bit—and brush it up and down on the wall until all the paint is off the brush. It will feel kind of dry when you're doing it because there's so little paint on the brush, but that's what you want. If there's too much paint on the wall, the area's going to be more likely to flash when light is on it and make the patch more visible once it's dry.

2   Keep repeating this process, using a little paint at a time, and you'll have a pretty smooth wall. Using long strokes that overlap each other will achieve the smoothest results.

Handy Ma'am Tip:

When it comes to brushes, make sure you're wetting a brush prior to using it. If you wet the brush prior to painting, the paint will come off easier and that paintbrush will have a longer life span. When you're cleaning the paintbrush, add a little bit of dish soap inside of the base and get up into the bristles as much as possible, then wash the brush out with hot soapy water. It's not uncommon for this to take minutes. You want all the paint you can see to be out of the brush, especially higher up inside of it because you want that paintbrush to last as long as possible. Quality paint brushes aren't cheap, so make sure you get your money's worth.

Handy Ma'am Tip:

If you'd like to blend the paint a little better, use a dry paintbrush. Once you've applied the paint with the first paintbrush, use this second paintbrush to go over the patch again and smooth the paint out along the edges. This helps eliminate extra paint along the edges and feather out the paint so it blends a little better.

PAINTING A WHOLE WALL

If you have multiple patches on a wall, I typically suggest painting the whole wall: corner to corner, corner to door frame, or door frame to door frame. This is because if you go all the way to the ceiling and all the way to the baseboard or all the way to the floor, that's going to give a good look and you're not going to notice you painted it. If you're trying to either match the previous paint from damages or if you're trying to do a whole new design, it's nice to be able to have that clean-looking finish.

PREPPING THE AREA

Before you begin, make sure to prep the space around the wall you'll be painting. When you're painting with a roller, you'll get some splatter, so you don't want to cause any damage to the floor or your things in the area.

If you have a hardwood floor, I don't recommend putting plastic down because that can slip. Use a canvas tarp instead. I always say go heavy duty because it's going to pay off in the long run. Apart from prepping the floor, make sure to cover with plastic anything that could potentially be damaged.

Remove anything attached to the wall, such as electrical outlet covers and light switch covers.

MATERIALS

dish soap, water, painter's tape (like FrogTape), and paint

1   Make sure to clean and dry the wall, frames, and baseboards with a little dish soap and water. Dry the wall well before applying tape. This will help the tape create a strong seal and prevent paint from leaking underneath it.

Handy Ma'am Tip:

Whether priming or painting, one of the things that's important to know is what size nap you need. Nap refers to the thickness of the texture on the paint roller itself. Typically, if you don't have much texture on your wall, you'll want a ¼-inch (0.65cm) nap and that's going to help you make sure the finish has no texture. If you have a textured wall, then you're going to want a ¾-inch (1.9cm) nap. Another thing to keep in mind is if you're really cautious about paint flying everywhere, especially with primer, using a shorter nap will help reduce the splatter. The thicker the roller cover, the more splatter you'll get.

2   Tape off everything you can with painter's tape. I always say it's best to go with FrogTape or other tapes that are a little bit more powerful to prevent leakage. If you're doing this for the first time, I recommend also putting painter's tape on the ceiling to give yourself a nice crisp edge on the wall. It's important to remember it can take you longer to prep a wall with painter's tape than to do the rest of the job, so if you're new to this, take your time with the prep.

3   Once you're ready to paint, you want to start with a primer, which is the first coat of paint. Primers tend to be a little bit more wet, so the paint is going to splatter a little more, so be mindful of this when working.

CUTTING IN

Before you start painting the entire section with a paint roller, you need to do something called "cutting in." This is when you paint along all the edges where you've taped as well as along any corners, frames, the ceiling, etc. This will give you a line along the edges so you don't have to roll too close with the roller and accidentally transfer paint to a surface you don't want it on.

The brush I prefer to use for this process is called a "shortcut brush." A shortcut brush has a smaller handle that fits strongly in your hand and it also has angled bristles.

If you're using latex paint, remember to use nylon brushes for the best result. Multipurpose brushes typically aren't the best and cheap throwaway brushes tend to leave a streaky finish and might even shed bristles.

Shortcut brush, paint

1 Load the brush with paint, making sure to get the paint inside the brush between the bristles. You want the bristles to be fully saturated with the paint.

2 Wipe both sides of the brush onto the paint can so the paint is still inside the brush but there's no excess on the outside.

3 Get the bristles right up against the edge you're cutting in—for example, along the ceiling. You want the paint on the wall but not on the ceiling, so place the brush on the wall where it meets the ceiling.

4 The bristles should be pressed up against the crease where you want the paint to go. Press lightly so they bend against the wall, creating a straight line. You don't want your bristles to go before your brush.

5 Drag the brush across the wall and apply a light amount of pressure to squeeze the paint out. This will push the paint into the edge, creating a nice straight line where the wall meets the ceiling (or whatever edge you're working on).

The farther you cut in, the more you can overlap with the roller later on and the more you can cover it all up and remove any streaks or brushstrokes. I always tell people that as soon as they're done cutting in to paint the wall. Don't wait too long; otherwise, it's going to have an uneven dry time and that could also cause some problems.

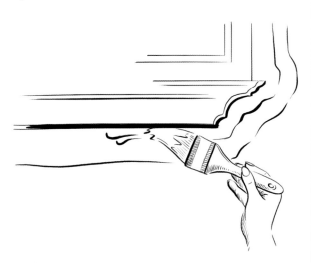

Handy Ma'am Tip:

Paint brushes come with a cover that's wrapped around the bristles. People often think this is just packaging they can throw away. Don't throw away that cover! It will keep the bristles for the paintbrush nice and straight. So use that once you're done painting.

PAINTING WITH A ROLLER

Now that you've got your edges cut in, it's time to break out the roller and cover the surface of the wall.

roller, roller cover, paint tray, paint

1   Pour the paint into the tray. Place the roller in the tray and get it saturated with paint.

2   As soon as you get it saturated, put the roller on the wall and start rolling the area. Start with 3-4-feet (91–122cm) sections.

3   Move the roller from the top down to the bottom. You want to do one long streak from the top to the bottom.

4   While you do this, put pressure on one end of the roller. You're essentially feathering it off and making one strong line down one side of the roller.

5   You're going to overlap the paint, so place the roller so its middle is on the line you just created. Bring your roller down again, once again placing pressure on the right side of the roller, moving the line farther down the wall.

6   What you're trying to do is make sure that line drags across the wall and keeps moving. So as you're each doing each section, that line should move farther down the wall until it either vanishes into a corner, vanishes into a door frame's trim, or is barely seen in darker lighting.

7   You're going to repeat that process over and over again until you get to the other end of the wall—and then you're done.

Once you are done with all the priming, then you can do the finish coat. The finish coat is essentially the same thing—you'll want to use the same techniques you were using in the previous steps, but now this is opening night rather than a dress rehearsal.

A finish coat tends to be thicker and doesn't flick as much paint. If you're doing a matched color, then the color you're matching is as close to the paint you have right now, so you probably don't need to get precise. If you're doing a different color, really think about the details and take your time. Use some of that artistic flare to help you make sure it blends into the wall as best as possible.

CLEANING A PAINTBRUSH OR PAINT ROLLER

One of the best tools I've ever gotten was a five-in-one tool. It has a curved edge on one side, which fits nicely around a paint roller and can scrape off the paint back into the bucket. That saves you money but also saves your sink.

When you're trying to clean out the roller, you can either choose to throw away the roller or try to clean it to use again. If you think you're going to do this job again soon or you're going to use the roller for another project you're working on, you can cover the roller with plastic to keep the paint wet for the next application.

SHELF IMPROVEMENT (MOUNTING, HANGING, AND ANCHORING)

HANGING FRAMES SAFELY

I always advise people to stay away from temporary hanging solutions that have a tendency to fall off the wall and cause damage. Products like Command strips can cause damage if used incorrectly, and while nails do make a puncture hole in your wall, they're very simple to repair.

Getting a picture hanger that can insert the nail at an 45° angle into the wall is going to be ideal. My preferred product is padded picture hangers. They have a padded hook on the back side and that helps them make sure that it's not damaging or nicking the wall when they're put on the wall.

For larger pictures that are above 30 pounds (14kg), Hercules hooks are extraordinarily effective. They leave only a very small insertion hole. They can be inserted into the wall with a puncture hole.

The quickest way to hang something on the wall if it has two hooks on the back or either side of the object is using painter's tape. You're going to use the tape to mark off where the hooks are on the object and then put the tape on the wall to mark off where those hooks are going to go. The tape is your template to where the hooks are.

1   Place a piece of painter's tape on the back of the object, making sure to have the tape level and placing it so it reaches across the object and just beyond each hook.

2   Use a pen or pencil to mark where the hooks are on the painter's tape.

3   Take the painter's tape off the object and place it on the level so it's flat along the top edge.

4   Put that level on the wall, making sure it's level by getting the center bubble in between the lines.

5   Find the marks you made on the tape and make a mark on the wall with a pencil in those same spots.

6   Make your holes with nails or screws, put the picture on the wall, and you're good to go!

Something as simple and as effective as that can go a long way toward making your home a little bit brighter and look nice and sharp.

USING MOUNTING TAPE

Many landlords and property management companies won't allow you to drill anything into the walls, which can make hanging things tricky. Using mounting tape or Command strips to hang things is an obvious option, but when used incorrectly, they can cause damage.

Here's how properly use mounting tape or Command strips:

- Plan to use them only for short periods of time (like a few months).

- Use the right size for your project: large surface area for smaller items; smaller surface area for smaller objects.

- Use on medium to lightly textured walls. More texture makes it harder to adhere.

- Properly prep the area, making sure it's clean and dry.

- Read the labels carefully. One side is meant for the wall, while the other side is meant for the object.

- Apply the tape to the object first, then press it firmly to the wall for at least a few seconds. (Read the label for specifics.)

Here's how to best remove mounting tape or Command strips:

- If the mounting tape has a tab, make sure to leave that on so you can use it to pull the tape off.

- If it doesn't have a tab, you'll need to pull a little off the wall to start, then pull it straight. You want to go in the direction opposite of the tape, away from the rest of the tape. If the tape is going up, pull down; if it's going right, pull left. If you pull it toward the direction of the tape, you might rip the drywall.

- Use a steamer to steam the area to warm it up quickly. This will help remove the adhesive and hopefully minimize damage.

Here are some additional tips for proper use:

- Avoid high-moisture areas, like the bathroom. The constant humidity over time will cause the adhesive to stick to the walls even more, making it likely it'll cause damage when being removed.

- Be careful when using mounting tape in really dry areas. It can lose adhesion more quickly and fall off. Check the mounting tape every three to six months to make sure it's still holding properly. Replace it with fresh tape when needed.

- Don't use mounting tape long term! After a year or two, it will cause damage from being up for so long.

- If you're painting a wall, wait a week or two to put any mounting tape on it. You want to let the paint cure before putting adhesive on it so it doesn't get damaged.

If you do damage the wall after using mounting tape or a Command hook, that's okay. It's totally normal! Refer to the drywall patch section on pages 108-109. It might not leave a hole, but you'll want to treat it like a hole if the top of the drywall has been stripped off.

REMOVING A NAIL

Removing a nail from the wall can be as simple as grabbing the tip with needle-nose pliers and pulling. But if it's nailed into a stud and it's not budging, then you might need to take the back of a hammer and use the claw to pull it out. If you apply that directly to the wall, you can dent the surface of the drywall, so you'll want to protect the wall.

MATERIALS

flat, hard surface (like a hardcover book or a piece of wood) and a hammer

1   Hold the hard surface up to the wall—just below the nail itself.

2   Place the claw side of the hammer on the hard surface and make sure the nail is in the claw.

3   Use the hard surface as leverage to pull the nail out. The hard surface will protect the wall while also helping you pull out the nail. The surface area of the hard object spreads out the pressure on the drywall and prevents damage.

USING DRYWALL ANCHORS

Drywall anchors come in all shapes, sizes, and styles. And people don't always understand how drywall anchors work, so let's talk about them. Drywall anchors are great substitutes for hanging lightweight to medium-weight things on your wall when you're not able to find the stud.

If you're trying to hang something wide, like a shelf, it's great to err on the side of caution and put at least one side of it on a stud and the other side on a drywall anchor. That helps with the weight distribution.

There are 3 types of drywall anchors I recommend the most:

- Toggle bolt wall anchor
- E-Z Anchor
- Colored plastic anchors (The color usually determines the weight it can hold.)

Handy Ma'am Tip:

It's okay for the metal toggle to drop behind the wall, and you can always get a new toggle to go with your bolts. Bits and pieces being dropped inside your drywall is super common and trust me when I tell you that when they were building your home, someone probably dropped screws and other things in there too.

TOGGLE BOLT WALL ANCHOR

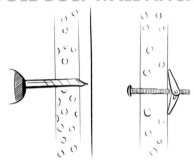

Toggle bolt wall anchors can be used for plaster walls and drywall. It requires a larger hole to be drilled with a bit and then inserted into the wall. Make sure the drill bit you use is just as wide as the toggle bolt itself when the bolt is closed.

Think of it like an alligator's mouth you're putting behind the wall. To do that, you'll start by screwing the screw into the toggle bolt so it looks like it's going into the mouth of the alligator. When you're inserting the alligator and the screw into the wall, the tail has to start going in first while the head and jaws are closed. Once you push the alligator all the way through, it's going to get mad at you and the jaws are going to open and come at you, but it's behind the wall. So when the jaws come at you, the alligator's mouth is going to get stuck in the drywall and not your hand!

These are great for using on ceilings, with mirrors and large picture frames, as hooks for hanging objects, and more. Because of the surface area that the toggle bolt wall anchor is going to cover, it's one of the strongest drywall anchors you can use. I highly recommend them. I love them and I think they're going to do you a lot of good.

If you have a toggle bolt wall anchor that's already inside the wall, you can remove it by taking the screw out and making sure the alligator mouth is taut against the wall. If the jaws of the alligator are pushed against the wall when you're taking the screw out, it will be easier to keep it from moving around inside the wall.

E-Z ANCHOR ANCHORS

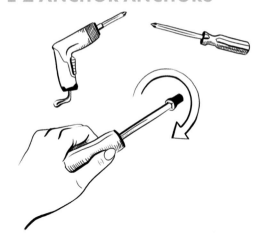

An E-Z Anchor anchor has two components: a screw and a stud. You'll use a Phillips screwdriver to screw the stud into the wall without using a drill. The flanges on the side of the stud will hold it strong in the drywall.

Put a screw into the center of the stud and the screw can hold whatever you need. This is a great option if you don't have a drill or aren't comfortable with a drill bit, like with the toggle anchor.

To remove an E-Z Anchor, remove the screw and then unscrew the stud with a Phillips screwdriver.

PLASTIC DRYWALL ANCHORS

The plastic drywall anchors you might see the most are white, blue, red, or green. The color denotes the strength of the anchor—how much weight it can hold up. The first thing you need to do is use the drill bit it often comes with. If it doesn't come with a drill bit, you need one that's just slightly bigger than the anchor itself. It's better to start small than to be oversized. You want it to be just snug enough to insert it into the hole you've created and then you can tap it in with a hammer.

You want to make sure you can get it ¾ of the way in before you hit it with a hammer; otherwise, you're going to break the drywall anchor. You can then insert the screw into the plastic once the anchor is firmly in the wall.

If you have a smaller plastic drywall anchor, the best way to remove that is by removing the screw and then using a drill bit to unscrew the anchor. You might occasionally need needle-nose pliers to remove the anchor, but the drill bit trick typically works.

SIZING A PLASTIC DRYWALL ANCHOR

The package of anchors will give you weight-bearing guidelines. All that's fine and dandy. However, those guidelines don't take into account how old your walls are or the thickness of your walls.

Drywall is still a fairly new thing in the industry. It's only been around for about a 100 years or so, and as it ages, we're discovering how brittle it can get. The guidelines on any drywall anchor package take only ideal circumstances into account. Always err on the side of caution and size up on an anchor. If you need it to hold 25 pounds (11kg), maybe get a 50-pound (23kg) anchor to be safe—or use two anchors.

FIXING A TOWEL RACK

A broken towel rack can be fixed in multiple ways. Towel racks usually have two pieces: the bar itself and some type of anchor or mount that goes on the wall.

This separate component–style often has a set screw underneath that can be released from the wall. The set screw can be hidden underneath the bar itself. There's sometimes a top cover that can be twisted off a little bit to reveal the set screw. But all the set screw essentially does is attach the anchors to the wall to hold up the towel rack.

If the rack is loose and pulling off the wall, take the set screw out and do one of the following:

- Tighten that drywall anchor or screw it down. It could have just wiggled itself loose over time.
- Put in a larger, more effective drywall anchor.

If the rack has pulled out from the wall and the hole isn't too large, the best fix is using a toggle bolt wall anchor (see page 121), especially if the hole is going to be covered up with the plate of the towel rack. The toggle bolt wall anchor is one of the strongest ones and it's really effective for towel racks because of how wide of a surface area it grabs behind the drywall.

If you've tightened all the screws or replaced them with the anchors and the towel rack keeps on getting loose, you might want to replace the anchor. There also could be something wrong with that specific location and finding a different location for the towel rack might be ideal because the drywall in that area could be too soft or old to hold the towel rack effectively. The placement of where that hole is might be making the problem worse, so you might have to fix that drywall patch and then put the towel rack somewhere else. (See pages 108–109 for fixing a drywall patch.)

PEEK-A-BOO BLINDS

REPAIRING BLINDS

Blinds in most apartments are actually mini blinds, which are notoriously prone to breaking, but the good news is that most mini blinds are replaceable. You can replace the individual components of them or you can replace the whole thing outright for a very affordable price.

If you only have one or two broken slats, it might be worth just replacing those. If you have a whole section—seven or more slats to replace—I recommend replacing the whole blind.

You can sometimes source individual slats online or in hardware stores. You can always take one slat to the store or take a picture with you to double-check the length, color, and size.

Another option is that when blinds are installed, they'll often come with extra slats. Apartment complexes will sometimes allow you to use the extra slats they have—either for free or for a cost. There might also be extra slats at the bottom of the blinds. If your blinds are much longer than your window, you can use some of those slats to replace broken ones.

REPLACING SLATS

flathead screwdriver,
needle-nose pliers or
tweezers, and scissors

1 Use a flathead screwdriver to remove the plastic plugs on the bottom rail.

2 There's a knotted string inside each hole called a lift cord. Use pliers to pull it out and untie the cord.

3 Pull each cord out of the bottom rail and continue to pull until it releases the number of slats you need at the bottom.

4 Remove the bottom rail and any extra slats out of the ladder (the sets of strings that are holding each slat) you might need.

5 Remove any damaged slats that need to be replaced and slide the new slats into the ladder, following the pattern of the slats that are already in the ladder.

6 Thread the bottom rail back through the ladder just below the last slat.

7 Thread each lift cord through the holes of the rail and tie a knot in each cord.

8 Use scissors to trim the ladder one rung below the bottom rail.

9 Use the flathead screwdriver to push the extra cords into the holes on the bottom rail.

10 Insert the plastic plugs back into the holes. The center of the ladder won't have extra lift cords.

11 If you removed quite a few of the undamaged slats at the bottom of the blinds, you might need to adjust the length of the cords. Begin by taking each cord stop and loosening the knots.

12 Slide the cord stops up the lift cord until they're 2–3 inches (5–8cm) below the top rail. Tighten the cord knots.

13 You might need to also adjust the tassels. Lift them up, tie new knots, and cut the excess cord from below the tassels.

REPLACING MINI BLINDS

When the old blinds have been removed or if they were missing to begin with, adding new blinds to your window is fairly easy. All models will be slightly different, so check the instructions before you begin, but this is a basic outline to follow universally. Regardless of the model, all mini blinds will have some type of bracket or mount for the wall.

Handy Ma'am Tip:

If your level isn't long enough to reach, attach a string to the top of your first bracket and bring it across the window. Place the string on top of the level and make sure the string is level to mark out where the second bracket will go.

MATERIALS

drill, tape measure, pencil or marker, flathead screwdriver, level, drywall anchors, and screws (I don't recommend using the ones that come with the blinds; they're often cheap and break or wear out quickly.)

1   Place the bracket on the wall and use a pencil or marker to mark where you want the screws to go.

2   If this is a replacement set of blinds, you're essentially trying to go into the similar but not identical location of the previous blinds so you're not using the holes that are already there. Blinds will either mount inside the window well or above it, so note where your original blinds were installed before removing them.

3   Mount the bracket to the wall by inserting the drywall anchor first and then screwing the bracket into the anchor.

4   Once you have the first bracket on the wall in your desired location, use the level to make sure the opposite side is even with the first bracket.

5   Place the blinds into the brackets and secure them.

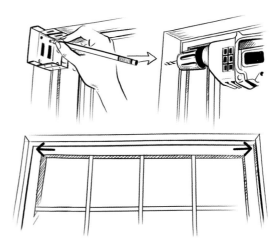

6   If there's a wand, you'll have to attach that after the blinds have been mounted. Hook the wand into the eye hook that's likely on the right side of the top rail.

Emotional Reset

Things like painting and hanging objects on a wall can make you feel like you're at home—they can make you feel like you belong a little bit more. Not having the opportunity to do those things because you're renting just seems like you're being robbed of feeling safe and loved in your own home. So I encourage having those conversations with your landlord when you first move in. Some landlords are really understanding; others aren't. Some will say explicitly in the lease that you can't do these things—and I leave it to you to know what's best for you and what you're willing to work with.

All these tasks are things you think you absolutely know how to do, but there are little tidbits that can help you have a little bit of an easier time. I still learn new things about tasks I've been doing for years and that's good. Knowledge should always be growing, reinforcing things, and should always help you look at a different perspective. And ultimately, you deserve to have a home that's a reflection of you and makes you feel seen and safe when you're relaxing and living your life.

DOORS, FLOORS, AND CABINETS

THE LOOSEY GOOSEY & NOT SO SCREWY SCREW HOLES

Be it on doorframes, doors, or cabinets, having a loose hinge because of a stripped screw hole is extremely frustrating. A stripped screw hole won't be able to hold the screw in place because the wood has worn out around it, causing a gap. This leaves nothing for the screw to attach itself to and it will begin to get loose or fall out. Adding a longer screw repeatedly can lead to cracked wood or damage to the area. The following is my way of fixing this nagging issue without having to entirely replace the wood. Note that as long as you're working with wood, this method can be carried out with many other applications.

Words to Know:

Pilot Hole: a small hole created with a drill bit prior to inserting a nail or screw in the same location. The hole removes a small amount of material, which prevents cracking and helps guide the nail/screw for more accurate placement. This is especially helpful for fragile or hard wood.

LOOSE SCREW HOLES

DIAGNOSING THE PROBLEM

- If the screw wiggles in the hole or can be pulled out without having to twist it, it might be time to refill those holes.

- If the screw wiggles but the wood around it is cracked, the following won't be the ideal fix for this situation and could lead to your having to replace the wood. If this is the case, you'll need to call the landlord and ask for a repair. (See page 42.). If you don't get a response, refer to the Tenant Resources chapter (page 209).

(See page 42.)
the Tenant Resources chapter (page 209).

MATERIALS

drill, toothpicks (or golf tees or wooden dowels), wood glue, scissors (or a serrated knife or small saw), and a hammer

1 Use your hand, a screwdriver, or a drill, remove the screw from the hole.

2 Rub wood glue on toothpicks (or use golf tees or wooden dowels).

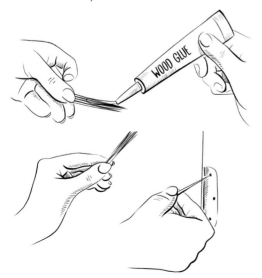

HOW DO YOU KNOW IF IT WORKED?

Once all the screws are in place, the hinge should be pressed firmly against the frame and not budge when the door moves. If this isn't the case, go back and repeat the steps, trying a thicker material. For example, if you used toothpicks the first time, you might try a dowel this time.

3 While the wood is still wet, place the toothpicks into the hole until they clump together and you can't fit any more in.

4 Snip or cut the toothpicks that are sticking out so a flat edge remains.

5 Use a hammer to lightly pound the toothpicks farther into the wood (being careful not to crack the wood).

6 Let the wood glue dry for 20 minutes to 1 hour.

7 To ensure you won't cause a crack in the wood, use a small drill bit to create a pilot hole in the desired location of the hole. A pilot hole is a small hole created with a drill bit prior to inserting a nail or screw in the same location. The hole removes a small amount of material, which prevents cracking and helps guide the nail/screw for more accurate placement. This is especially helpful for fragile or hard wood.

8 Screw the screw back into the hole (and through the hinge if one exists).

REPLACING A BROKEN LATCH OR DOORKNOB

From time to time, if the latch of a door (that's the pokey thing that comes out of the door) isn't properly lined up with the strike plate, the latch itself can go bad. The latch pushes in when you turn the knob, and when it goes inside of its mechanism inside the door, it's pressed up against everything. That latch is all that keeps the door from swinging open when you're just inside a room or inside your home. And when you turn that knob, then the door can open. That's the simple mechanism—it's just hiding inside this little hole.

Latches have various components to them that can cause problems. The latch itself can get a little bit loose, and if that happens, it's not going to have the tension it needs to go in and out. There's also a square mechanism that's inside of it. If you take the whole knob off and you look at the mechanics inside, the square bit is actually what turns it in. That square hole is what holds the knobs together. And when you turn the knob, it grabs the latch inside the knob and then pulls it inward. If that cracks, it's one of the leading causes of a latch not latching anymore. The simplest way to solve this problem is just replacing the knob and the mechanics altogether.

MATERIALS

Phillips screwdriver, new door latch or entire doorknob kit

Handy Ma'am Tip:

Take a photo of each step as you take apart doorknobs so you can replace them the exact same way.

1   Take the screws out of the current latch. There are two on the latch plate that you'll find on the edge of the door.

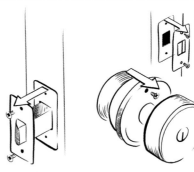

2   Remove the inside door handle by unscrewing it or you might have to pop off the doorknob itself by pushing in the pin with the screwdriver first to expose the screws or remove any plate attached. Set aside those components.

3   The exterior doorknob will have been screwed into the interior side, so that should come off easily with the interior doorknob.

4   The latch should now be removable from inside the doorknob hole.

5   You've now taken apart the entire doorknob and you can either replace the latch or install a new doorknob kit. Make sure to follow any specific instructions from the manufacturer.

6   Insert the new latch and screw the plate in place on the edge of the door.

7   Make sure the rounded edge of the latch faces towards the door so that when it hits the strike plate, it pushes the latch in and allows the door to close. If the straight edge is facing the door, when you go to close it, the straight edge will hit the strike plate and prevent the door from closing.

8   Place the exterior doorknob on, making sure the lock is on the correct side, and hold it in place.

9   Place the interior doorknob back on and make sure the screw holes line up with the other side.

10 Screw the doorknob plates into place.

11 Replace any cover plates or knobs and you should be good to go!

FIXING A LOOSE DOORKNOB

Loose doorknobs can be a pain, making it so it's difficult for you to enter a room or sometimes causing you to get stuck (or even worse, your kids get stuck because they can't turn the doorknob to get out of a room). Replace a loose doorknob as soon as possible to keep everyone safe. It's a really easy fix and should only take a few minutes with the right materials.

MATERIALS

flathead screwdriver, Phillips screwdriver, and silicone caulking

1 Some doorknobs will have exposed screws, but if you can't see the screws on yours, you'll likely have a pin located on the side of the doorknob you can push in with a flathead screwdriver. Push it in and pop off the plate on the door to reveal the screws underneath.

2 Take out one screw and leave the rest for now so the knob components remain on the door.

3 Put silicone caulk on the screw and rub it into the threads.

Handy Ma'am Tip:

I don't recommend using Loctite or another permanent screw adhesive for this because you want to be able to remove the screws if you ever need to fix or replace a doorknob again.

4 Screw the screw back into the hole.

5 Repeat this process with any remaining screws.

6 Make sure all the screws are nice and tight.

7 Place the cover back on.

8 Put the knob back on by pushing in the pin while you put it in place. It should click into place.

Check the doorknob a few times to make sure it's tight enough but not too tight—and you're good to go.

FIXING A STRIKE PLATE

The strike plate is the metal plate on the doorframe that your door latch goes into when it's closed. It can often get wonky over time and prevent your latch from being able to go into the hole correctly, making it so the door doesn't stay closed.

DIAGNOSING THE PROBLEM

- Check the door when it's closed to make sure the hinges aren't loose.
- Check to make sure the door isn't misaligned. There should be even spacing all around the door in the doorframe.
- If the door isn't level or the hinges are loose, refer to how to fix a hinge (page 130).
- On the latch, put chalk, lipstick, or something that will rub off easily when the door closes.

- Close and open the door a few times.
- You should see the chalk rub off on the strike plate, and if the mark is too high or too low, you'll want to move the strike plate.

You might notice I don't often use proper terminology when we're talking about these jobs—and the reason why is because I feel like you as a person doing the job and me explaining it don't need the proper terminology to be able to understand what we're talking about. And at the end of the day, I'm not trying to make you a professional. I'm trying to get the job done along with you! So don't feel silly if you don't know the names. I know that with just a little bit of patience, you'll be doing a great job with this. Good for you!

MOVING THE STRIKE PLATE

Phillips screwdriver, chisel (or another sharp/flat object), and a hammer or mallet

1 Remove the screws holding the strike plate in place.

2 Place the strike plate on the doorframe in a way that puts the latch right in the center of it.

3 Mark around the plate with a pencil. This is what will need to be removed. You should only have to remove the part of the frame that the strike plate goes onto. There should be a large enough hole for the latch. If not, use a chisel and hammer to carve out the spot you marked.

4 If the new screw holes are too close to the old ones, you'll want to seal those old holes first using the toothpick method. (See page 131.) If the old screw hole is too small for toothpicks, you can drill a slightly larger hole and fill it in.

5 Once you've filled in the old holes, you can screw the strike plate into the new space you created.

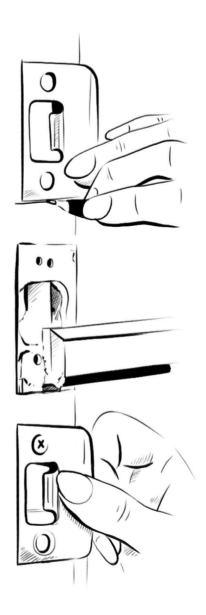

REPAIRING A LOCK

Locks in your home take on a lot of work and there are pins and mechanisms inside there that can go bad over time. When the lock itself gets tight, your reaction is to spray good old WD40 inside there, which will initially work. But over time, because it's a petroleum-based substance, it's going to grab dust, debris, and particles from the air, creating a bigger problem down the road. Instead, use something called graphite powder or silicone spray. These items are great because they're essentially dry lubricants that will reduce friction without causing future issues.

MATERIALS

graphite powder or silicone spray

1 Squirt graphite powder or silicone spray inside the lock, then take the key and move it in and out a few times to distribute the lubricant.

2 If it starts budging, that's great. If not, redo this process a few more times until it's loosened up.

3 Make sure you wipe the key off the first couple times you're using it because there will be some debris left behind.

If this method doesn't work, then you'll need to replace the lock. If you're in a rental unit, that's not something you can do without the permission of the landlord, so put in that work order ASAP! Your safety should be considered an emergency, so make sure to let them know to respond to you quickly.

Handy Ma'am Tip:

Keep your face a good distance away from graphite powder when using it or wear a mask because it's very fine and you don't want that to go down your throat.

CLEANING OR REPLACING A PEEPHOLE

If you have a peephole that's dirty or broken and you can't see out of it, this can be bad for security reasons, so let's get it fixed. If the door is painted, you might need an X-acto knife to score around the peephole and release it from the paint before removing it.

MATERIALS

flathead screwdriver, butter knife, or a sturdy card. If those don't work, you can put masking tape around the peephole ring to protect your door and then use a small pair of adjustable pliers.

1   The peephole will have a ring on the inside of the door with two notches across from each other on that ring. Those notches are what will help you turn the ring to unscrew the peephole. You need something that can reach across the peephole and catch both of those notches to get enough torque to turn it, like a butter knife, sturdy card, or large flathead screwdriver. If that doesn't work, use masking tape and adjustable pliers to wrap the ring with tape, hold the ring with the pliers, and turn the ring.

2   Spin it out lefty loosey and that will loosen up the screws inside because it's just one big screw with glass on the inside and facing outside. Your door is acting as the meat in between the sandwich—this peephole sandwich—and your peephole is the bread going on either side and through the middle like a double decker.

3   You can now clean the peephole with vinegar or any type of soap and a little bit of water. That should be all you need to do. If you need to replace the peephole, move on to installing a new peephole.

4   When you're finished, put the clean or new peephole back into its hole, with the notches on the inside and glass on the outside.

5   Use a butter knife or the pliers to twist righty tighty to screw the peephole into place. And then you're good to go!

REPAIRING A SLIDING CLOSET DOOR

The sliding closet door—woo! These can be a nightmare. I'm pretty sure everyone has experienced that moment when the door just comes right off the track. (The track is the metal casing that's screwed into the doorframe—on top of the door.) Here's the simple fix I've done many times and I highly recommend it. Essentially, what you're going to do is take the old track and make it a bypass door.

How it should work: You have a door and a rail, and 2 brackets with wheels on the top of each door. On the floor is a plastic guide that keeps the doors from swinging out. Often the guide breaks, or the doors are too high from the guide, and the guide fails. The door will swing out now and the brackets and wheels will easily come off the rail, making the door fall off. What we'll be doing is adding a screw to the top to create a homemade top-guide to prevent the door from swinging out enough to fall off.

MATERIALS

four hex head screws or leg screws (the larger the head, the better), drill, and a crescent wrench

1. Take the door off to begin by finding and loosening the screws on the back of the door at the top. They attach the hanging mechanism to the door. It will now be loose enough to pull the door from the bottom and wiggle it to get the rollers off the top track.

2. Drill a pilot hole (see page 130) the same size as the screw into the top of the door. You'll want to make a hole just on the outside of where the roller will be—on the left and right sides of the top of the door and just off the center of the edge.

3. Screw the hex screws all the way in and put the door back on the track, tightening up the hanging hardware again.

4. Use a crescent wrench to unscrew one of the hex screws a bit so it comes up out of the pilot hole high enough to hold the door on the track. Repeat on the other side.

Handy Ma'am Tip:

If you're able to install new closet doors, I recommend a double bypass door because it will make it impossible for it to come off the rail!

What you're doing is putting the screw right on the top edge of the door so the screw is essentially going to sit on the outer side of the rail. The wheel is going to sit on the inside of the rail and the screw's going to be on the outside. It's hugging it like a sandwich. This is going to prevent the door from swinging out when your kids or anybody's just having a good time!

If you still need help with the door, you also might want to look into replacing the plastic slider holder on the bottom of the floor. This is called a sliding closet door bottom guide. You can find metal ones that are online for about $4. All you'll need is two screws that go into the floor. This is a great little trick, and if you originally had plastic ones, they get beaten up, so I highly recommend just getting a $4 one. And you're good to go!

Handy Ma'am Tip:

You can even use a Sharpie to mark off where the screws are going to go before you take the door off the track. Make sure you're just going on the other side of the track. You might not be able to see it, but you're going to use a Sharpie on the top of the door and mark the screw spots at the very top where that rail is. Then when you take the door off, you'll know exactly where to drill those pilot holes.

FIXING BIFOLD CLOSET DOORS

A bifold door is a door that essentially folds in half as it is pushed toward the frame of the door, creating more space to access your closet vs. a single sliding door.

MATERIALS

vise-grip pliers (or channel locks or flathead screwdriver), and a hammer

1 Find the spring roller that's on top of the door you want to remove, located at the center of the track.

2 Push down the spring to release that side of the door. The door will still be hanging on the second spring that's located on the frame of the closet.

3 Grab the door and push it upward. This will release the spring on top and allow you to pull it toward you to slide it out. The bottom spring will also release when you do this, allowing you to remove the entire door from the frame.

4 One of the rollers on the top of the door will often go bad and get chipped away or cracked. To take the old roller out, use vise-grip pliers or even a flathead screwdriver to apply pressure on the outward sides of it to pull it out. Use a hammer to lightly tap a new roller into the existing hole.

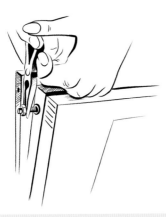

Handy Ma'am Tip:

These instructions are for a double bifold door on a long closet, but they can easily be used for a single bifold door. Instead of following instructions for the center of the track, you'll simply focus on the opposite side of the door that rolls back and forth, not the stationary side.

5 Sometimes, the issue isn't the roller and it's a damaged or bent track instead. The track is the metal casing that is screwed into the doorframe, both on top and on the floor beneath the door.

6 If the track is bent or broken in any way, you can remove the two screws that are holding up the track and then bend it back to make sure it's as even as possible.

7 You can also leave the track hanging up and use pliers to bend it in shape. This metal is typically cheaper and easier to mold, so keep that in mind when you're doing it to make sure you don't snap it off.

8 These tracks are also fairly easy and affordable to replace if that's the route you need to go.

9 After replacing the parts you need or fixing the track, then you should be ready to put the door back in. Put the bottom spring in the track first.

10 Slide in the top spring that's on the frame side. You might want to use a flathead screwdriver to push it down to get it in easily.

11 Push the center roller down a little bit, slide it into the track, and let it go. The door should go right into a slot with a little bit of wiggle and then you're good to go.

FIXING AN IMPROPERLY HUNG CABINET DOOR

Cabinet doors nowadays typically have a little locking mechanism in the back of the hinge that you can use to remove the door without any tools or needing to unscrew the door.

Cabinet doors usually have two hinges. On the back side of each hinge is a little tab. There are also two screws on these tabs. The one that's farther away from you will allow you to adjust the hinge to slide in and out.

So if your cabinet door is a little bit too far away from the rest of the cabinet, you can tighten it up and that will bring it in. And if you loosen it up, it will push it out so if the door is a little too tight, it will give you more space. You'll sometimes also notice that the top and bottom hinges aren't level with each other. One might be farther out or closer in, making the door appear crooked. You can adjust the way the door hangs by adjusting the screws on both hinges. A little bit of adjustment to the top hinge or a little bit of adjustment to the bottom hinge can help even out the door itself.

The other screw that's closer to you is the one that adjusts the door away from the side of the wall. So that closest screw is pushing it either farther away from the wall and toward the other door or closer to the wall away from the other door. So if you have a large gap between the doors or the doors are hitting each other when you close them, you can fix that by adjusting the screws on one or both of the doors.

If for any reason you need to remove the doors completely—to clean, paint, etc.—you can also use these tabs so you don't have to take the hinges completely off the door or cabinet. To remove the doors, follow these steps:

1 Make sure to have a firm grip on the door so it doesn't fall when you release the hinge.

2 Grab the tab with your thumb and forefinger, squeeze, and pull it toward you.

3 This will release the hinge. Repeat for the second hinge to remove the door completely.

There might also be a screw in the back you can loosen and take off, but it's usually a tab. With that tab, you can take the cabinet door right off and do some of these repairs a little more easily.

REPAIRING AND PATCHING A HOLE IN A DOOR

There are many reasons why a hole could be created in a door—and some of those reasons can be kind of scary. Over the years working in property management, I've seen some pretty awful situations. If you feel unsafe in your home, please reach out to people you already know or local organizations that can help. You should not be dealing with this situation alone. It's not normal for people to be treated this way.

That being said, there are also very accidental reasons for a hole in a door. First, assess the damage. If you have severe damage to the door, if it's peeling, it's coming off its hinge, or the hole is larger than a foot, I recommend replacing the door. That's not something I'm going to show in this chapter, but it's something I'd recommend. But if it's a crack, gouge, or a small hole, then I recommend doing the trick I'm going to show you now.

MATERIALS

expanding spray foam (I recommend Great Stuff), utility knife, Bondo putty, putty knife, sanding block, paint to match the door, and painting supplies

Disclaimer:

If you're in an apartment and your door isn't painted already, the door isn't white, or the door is fake wood or anything along those lines and you are wondering what to do, you can often get away with painting the door white. If other doors in the home are already white or you've been there for several years, your landlord might not notice. I don't highly recommend it, but it's a route you can go.

1   Spray the expanding foam inside the hole, then allow it to expand for a little bit. It usually takes about a day. If the expanding foam is just going inside the door itself because you have a hollow door, you can take little pieces of cardboard and make a circle inside the hollow door to encase the hole and create a barrier for the foam. Adhere the cardboard with hot glue. You're just building a border, to trap the expanding foam.

2   Use a utility knife to cut off any foam that has expanded beyond the outside of the door. You're using the expanding foam to create more strength underneath the patch.

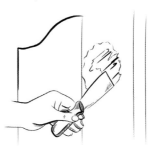

3   Once the foam has set, then it's time to apply the Bondo. You want to mix the Bondo well and make sure it has a consistent color. Use a putty knife to layer it on and spread it on all the sides first and then the center of the hole itself. This can take up to three, four, and sometimes more coats, but once you get it on there, it will set fairly quickly. Make sure to do nice, smooth strokes down in one direction.

4   Once it's all dry, then you can take a large sanding block and sand off all the sides and the rough edges.

5   Paint the door and then you're good to go!

REPAIRING CORRUGATED CARPET

This fix is really simple and is great for runs in corrugated carpet. Corrugated carpet is often builder's-grade material because it easily hides imperfections. It feels raised and bumpy when you touch it, and as long as you can walk by without noticing it, you should be fine!

MATERIALS

superglue or hot glue, and a flathead screwdriver

Handy Ma'am Tip:

If needed, you can sometimes find pieces of carpet in the back of the closet to repair the patch.

1   Apply glue to the mesh that the carpet got pulled out of.

2   Use a flathead screwdriver to push the carpet back into the mesh.

3   Take your time and apply more glue as needed.

4   Go back and forth over the carpet run with the flathead to blend it into the carpet.

REPAIRING AND REPLACING BASEBOARDS

There are two types of baseboards: vinyl and wood. Vinyl baseboards are flexible and usually attached with adhesive. Wood baseboards are sturdy and attached with nails.

VINYL BASEBOARDS

If you have vinyl baseboards that begin falling off the wall in your rental, there are two easy ways to fix them. For both methods, you'll be applying cove base adhesive on the back of the vinyl baseboard.

MATERIALS

vinyl baseboard strips and cove base adhesive

1   You can replace a vinyl baseboard entirely. Cut vinyl strips to size. Apply a cove base adhesive to the strips to attach them to the wall. Apply pressure to ensure they're fully secured.

2   You can also simply fix the peeling vinyl baseboard if it's just a small part. You don't even need to remove the entire baseboard for this method—just peel the baseboard back a little bit, put some adhesive on the back of it, and then press it against the wall.

WOOD BASEBOARDS

A wood baseboard is also easy to fix or replace. Just follow these instructions.

MATERIALS

ruler, flat saw, nail gun, wood putty, and paint

1   Measure out how much replacement baseboard you need. Use a ruler and pencil to draw a straight vertical line and cut the replacement baseboard with a flat saw.

2   Use a nail gun to adhere the baseboard to the studs, fill in the nail holes with wood putty, and paint the baseboard.

3   Some baseboards also have what's called quarter round attached to it at the floor. (It looks like a rounded piece of wood that's separate from the baseboard itself.) If your baseboards have this, you'll also have to replace that.

If these tricks don't seem to work, you can get double-facing tape or double-sided tape. Carpet tape works especially well for this because it has microfibers in there and it's very strong—it will hold up against the wall. All you have to do is pull off the area that's having the problem, put some carpet tape on there, cut off the excess, and then put the baseboard back on. And there you go!

Handy Ma'am Tip:

It's great if you have anti-stick scissors. They're ideal for carpet and I highly recommend getting yourself a pair—they're worth the investment!

REPAIRING HARDWOOD FLOORING

If you have significant damage to hardwood flooring or have boards that need to be replaced, please don't try to fix these issues yourself! There might be some loss of your deposit, but you could get into more issues trying to cover up larger issues with your floor.

If you have a small chip in the floor, some small discolored spots, or a little bit of the floor has pulled up from the subfloor, those are manageable repairs.

First and foremost, if you have a chip in the floor, keep the broken piece because it might come in handy. Chips usually happen because the floor is pulling up from the subfloor. You need to reattach the wood to the subfloor before you can replace the chip. You'll know this is the case if the board that got chipped isn't level with the rest of the floor.

MATERIALS

drill, polyurethane, and a wood screw

1   Pre-drill a pilot hole (see page 130) in the floor where the chip is missing.

2   If there's exposed raw wood, put the pilot hole through that—but go nice and slow.

3   Put some polyurethane inside that hole.

4   Put a wood screw through the polyurethane and into the pilot hole. Drill the wood screw into the wood, making sure it catches the subfloor.

Handy Ma'am Tip:

If you have a countersink drill bit, the screw will go into the hole more, which can be a better and stronger solution. This drill bit has a countersink on it, which helps push a screw deeper, allowing the hole to be filled.

5   Place some wood glue on that raw wood to cover the screw.

6   Place the chip back in its slot and hold it there until it dries, about a minute or so.

7   Wipe away all the excess glue so you don't see it as noticeably. It might not look perfect, but it will get the job done for you.

8   You can always use a little bit of wood filler and then use a stain that matches the color of the floor.

Make sure to stand up when you're done and do a walk-by test. If you can't see the chip when you're walking by it, then you're good to go!

REPAIRING A CHIP IN LAMINATE FLOORING

Laminate flooring is common in apartments because it's typically cheaper than hardwood floors. I'm not going to talk about a full replacement for laminate flooring because again, this is much more taxing and it's costly, so I don't recommend renters get into that themselves. But when it comes to chips, that's something you can do.

You can use something called a color wax for small repairs. You're going to need the right color for the flooring. You can check for different options online or in a hardware store.

MATERIALS

colored wax, utility knife or putty knife, parchment paper, iron, and a blow-dryer

1 Color wax will need to be warm. To do this, set an iron on its lowest temperature possible. Place the parchment paper on top of the wax, then move the iron across the parchment paper.

2 Once the wax is pliable, carefully remove the parchment paper. Don't burn yourself.

3 Remove all the extra debris in the chipped area and make sure it's cleaned out well and dry.

4 Use a utility knife or a putty knife to shave a little piece of wax. Work it into the chipped laminate. You want to fill this hole the best you can because you don't want water to get underneath it and rot the subfloor.

5 Once you get the wax into the chipped spot, use a blow-dryer to mold and smooth the wax. Remove any excess wax with a little bit of water.

6 As you inspect your work, if you feel like the wax has sunk down a little bit, once it gets a little harder, you can add more layers on top.

Emotional Reset

When I started writing this book, I knew there were things I wasn't going to be able to tell every single person. The fact is, everything is going to have a different repair or there are going to be different things every person encounters. It's impossible to give you a universal method to fix all the things in your home. And I'd never want to lead you down a path where that's the thing you could believe.

Because when it comes to me as a professional, there are often things that I'm googling or looking for on YouTube to learn all the time. I never stop! And a lot of the repairs in this chapter were things I'd learned during a period of my life when I didn't know the answers either. But I never stopped myself from learning because I thought I knew how to repair something. Sometimes, it wasn't enough for me to think I knew how to repair something. I had to check and recheck my knowledge and work.

By doing this, I ended up learning more than my peers. So don't let the idea of "I know enough to solve a problem" get in the way of pursuing more knowledge. You can never have enough knowledge with this stuff. When it comes to so many of these repairs—from all the tips and tricks to different ways to be able to solve problems—there might be something you can learn from somewhere else out there, not just from me!

Never let that stop you. Never let this be a roadblock for you. I'm proud of you for continuously learning and I'm proud of you for attempting and reattempting something because that's how we get better. And I'm proud of you for doing the best you can.

ELECTRICAL REPAIRS

BEFORE YOU BEGIN: A SAFETY DISCLAIMER

In an ideal world, an electrical technician will be the one doing all the work I discuss in this chapter because these repairs can ultimately be really scary. Also, you don't want to do this work if you're not a licensed electrician. Landlords and maintenance technicians should be taking care of this work—but certainly not you.

But we often don't live in an ideal world. So I'm arming you with information to understand how this work is done. Remember, a lot of information in this section is about things that can cause severe harm and danger as well as be life threatening. I don't believe in sugarcoating things like this, so I want to let you know I've shocked myself when doing electrical work before. Once again, I don't endorse doing this work yourself, but having the knowledge is still very important to be able to discuss with your technician or know what needs to be fixed or replaced.

LABELING BREAKER BOXES

When you first move into an apartment, one of the very first things I'd suggest you do is go to your electrical box and label it. Additionally, when you're moving in your furniture, take care not to place anything in front of outlets or switches. It's difficult to check outlets, switches, etc., when you have a bed or a couch or something else in the way.

Once the breaker has been labeled, you'll know exactly what room to turn off the power to in the case of an emergency. How do you know which breaker is for which room in your home? Checking the breakers with somebody who's an expert is going to make the process a whole lot easier. If you're doing it alone, there are two ways to go about it:

- Plug an old FM radio or something else that makes noise into an outlet in any room. Turn off a breaker one by one—or simply test the ones you think it might be—and when you hear the device turn off or go silent, you know that the outlet is with that breaker.
- You can also use a lamp. Make sure the lamp is situated so you can see it turn off when you're using the breaker. You can also turn off the breaker, walk into the room, and see if the lamp is on or not. This can feel time consuming, but it's worth the effort.

Just to be sure, you should test more than one outlet in every room, typically ones that are across from each other. If they're next to each other, they're often on the same breaker. If you have empty breakers at the end of your testing, then you can go back and test each one once more to find it.

Another option is to use outlet testers, which plug right into your outlet and can help you find the associated breaker. Typically, the breakers are broken down into different sections in your home. One breaker will often cover an entire bathroom, another breaker will cover a kitchen, etc. Appliances, like dishwashers or dryers, will use two breakers together. This is a larger circuit and that's why the breaker will look bigger.

Most electrical breakers will also have a little label spot so you can put in a card or put in a piece of paper. If it doesn't, you could just write on a piece of notebook paper or print it off on a computer and then adhere it to the inside of your electrical breaker. This will save you and an electrician a lot of time in the future.

ELECTRICAL OUTLET REPAIRS

INSTALLING OUTLET SPACERS

If you have an outlet that's embedded too far into the wall and it seems to be cracking the outlet cover every single time you try to plug something in, then you might have an outlet that needs to have spacers added to it. Spacers are relatively inexpensive and can be found at most hardware stores.

MATERIALS

flathead screwdriver, Phillips screwdriver, and outlet spacers

1 Turn off the associated breaker for the outlet you need to repair. Make sure no one in the home goes near the breaker while you're working, and no one is using any electrical items in the house while you're turning the breaker on and off.

2 At the outlet, use a flathead screwdriver to remove the outlet cover.

Handy Ma'am Tip:

I always tell people to act like an outlet is hot even when it's not. This mean that even when you know an outlet is off and you know there's no power going to the outlet, still err on the side of caution.

3 Remove the two screws holding the outlet in the junction box. Those are typically Phillips but sometimes flathead.

4 Pull out the outlet to allow just a little of the cords to come out and with enough room to add the spacers.

5 Fold the spacers in half and place them one at a time into the outlet. Put the outlet back into place and test that the outlet doesn't go beyond the flush of the wall but is out farther than before. You might not get a proper fit right away, so be patient with yourself as you add or remove spacers until the outlet fits just right.

6 Screw the outlet back into place and screw the cover back on.

7 Plug in the outlet tester, a radio, or a lamp. Turn on the breaker to turn on the power and verify that the outlet works.

OUTLET REPLACEMENT

If a plug keeps falling out of an outlet, then a simple fix is to replace the outlet.

new outlet, flathead screwdriver, Phillips screwdriver, and electrical tape

1 See page 151 for how to remove the outlet cover. Before following the step to remove the outlet, check the outlet to see whether you need a 15-amp outlet or a 20-amp outlet. Replace the outlet cover. Continue with these steps once you've bought the needed outlet.

2 If you haven't already labeled the circuits in your breaker box, see page 150 for how to do this. Turn off the breaker associated with the outlet you need to replace.

3 Remove the outlet cover again. You should have about 3-6 inches (8-15cm) of wire.

Handy Ma'am Tip:

Take a picture of the old outlet to see how it's wired just in case. Don't remove all the wires at once. Remove one wire at a time and place it into the new outlet so you don't lose track or get confused.

4 Unscrew the wires from the old outlet and match them to the same plugs on the new outlet, screwing them into place on the new outlet. In the United States, the typical connections are the white wire to the silver nut, the black wire to the bronze nut, and the green wire to the green nut. If you don't see a green wire, STOP what you're doing and put in a maintenance request. The green wire is for grounding and it's what keeps you safe from electrocution. Not having that wire indicates there might be something wrong. Put the outlet back in and let your technician know that the green wire is missing.

5 Once all the wires are connected, give each one a gentle tug to make sure they're securely in place and won't come loose when you put the outlet back into the wall.

6 If the electrical box in your wall is metal (usually silver), wrap electrical tape around the back of the new outlet—around the metal—to further secure the wires as well as prevent further problems inside the wall. If your box is plastic (usually blue), wrapping is not required.

7 Put the new outlet back into the wall, screw the outlet into place, and screw the cover over the outlet.

8 Turn the breaker back on and see page 151 for how to ensure the new outlet works.

If you encounter any problems and the outlet still isn't working, I highly advise you to reach out to a professional to do this because you won't know for sure if the breaker is still on or not. If something's wrong, I don't advise just shoving the outlet back in there and trying to get it working before you turn on the breaker again.

If you turn off the breaker and you don't know for sure if that outlet is off when you're working on it, use a multimeter to tell for sure that it's off. But I don't recommend using a non-contact voltage tester (it looks like an electrical wand) because that can sometimes give a false reading or not give a reading at all when there should be—and not knowing whether the outlet is truly off can put your life in danger. When working with electricity, always err on the side of caution!

Handy Ma'am Tip:

If you're concerned about working on electrical or just need a quick fix until you can do the full repair, I recommend the Snug Plug. It's a small piece of plastic that goes into the part of the outlet the electrical prongs go into and it helps your electrical plug fit more snugly into the outlet so it doesn't fall out!

LITTLE LIGHT FIXES

REMOVING A BROKEN BULB

If you have a broken bulb in a light socket, that can be a terrifying thing to see and dangerous to try to fix. But don't be scared—let's take it one step at a time.

MATERIALS:

half a potato, clothespin, and a socket expansion tool

1   Turn off the light switch associated with the light socket. See page 150 for how to turn off the breaker that controls that light socket.

2   If the filament—the center of the bulb—is still intact and pointed out, push a half a potato into the filament and gently twist lefty loosey until the broken bulb comes out.

3   If no filament is poking out, insert a clothespin into the metal cup of the bulb. Expand the clothespin, which should provide enough tension to allow you to turn the bulb lefty loosey to remove it.

4   If you don't have a clothespin, use a socket expansion tool to remove the bulb. This tool is designed for just this purpose. Simply insert it like you would the clothespin, expand it, and then twist lefty loosey to pull out the bulb.

REMOVING A BROKEN MOUNTED LIGHT

A lot of you renters will recognize this fixture: It's a ceiling-mounted light most commonly known as the boob light! Removing the cover to replace a bulb that's burnt out can be difficult. There are usually three different ways the cover is attached to the fixture, so I'll explain how to remove each type.

adjustable pliers or wrench, Allen key, flathead screwdriver, and a Phillips screwdriver

- **Screw-in cover:** This kind of cover has grooves that allow it to screw into place. This can often trap moisture, making it hard to remove the cover. Grip the cover with both hands, push upward, and turn the cover lefty loosey. If necessary, use a little force—a good jolt can help remove the cover.

- **Nut and bolt:** At the center of the cover is a nut you can typically turn lefty loosey with your hand to remove the cover. If this proves tricky, you can use pliers or a wrench to remove the nut.

- **Side screws:** On the sides of the cover are set screws (usually more than one and often up to three) you can remove with an Allen key, a flathead screwdriver, or a Phillips screwdriver. These screws can be hard to find because of their placement, but take your time and ensure you prevent the cover from crashing to the ground, especially if it's a glass one.

REMOVING A RECESSED FIXTURE

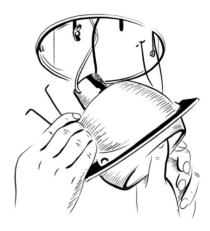

Many recessed fixtures have a glass cover that can be unscrewed to reveal a reflector inside that needs to be removed to actually get to the bulb itself. You can pull down the reflector and on the two sides are essentially antennas.

When these antennas are far apart, tension is applied into the slots the antennas are inserted into. If you pull those antennas in and make them look more like rabbit ears, then you can pull them down and then replace a bulb. Reinsert the rabbit ears, expand them again, and put everything back together.

REPAIRING FLICKERING LIGHT BULBS

If a light bulb flickers or randomly turns on or off, it's typically a bulb that's ready to go out. Older bulbs and incandescent bulbs have a filament inside. When these kinds of bulbs are ready to go out, they'll start flickering or randomly turn on or off. LED lights often will do the same. When you see that flickering, it's time to replace the bulb because it's harder to do if the light goes out in the dark.

FLUORESCENT TUBE LIGHTS

If you have fluorescent tubes in your home, which are getting rarer these days, there are a few things you'll want to know when dealing with them:

- Their covers are typically made out of plastic and they're diffuser covers that serve a purpose: expanding the light in the given area.
- The light fixture cover causes that expansion of light, but that cover itself can get really brittle and fragile over time because of the hot flex tubes. That heat makes the plastic dry out, causing it to easily break and crack. When you're removing the cover, be careful and patient.
- Every single light fixture like this will have a different mechanism for access to it, but they often use tension on the sides—almost like a bear hug around the light fixture.
- There can also be little latches on the side that can be pulled up to release the cover.
- Either way, caution is important here so you don't damage the cover because they're becoming harder and harder to replace.

If the fluorescent tubes are flickering and look like they're having a great time in a disco bar in the 1970s, then those tubes are on their way out and need to be replaced. Essentially, you'll see black spots on the side of a fluorescent tube. Those spots are basically mercury vapor—mercury vapor mixed with rayon, no puns intended. And every time the light is turned on, that heats up the bulbs, which moves the gas around the tubes to make light.

The potential for a tube to go out sooner rather than later is because of several possibilities, which can result in a bad discharge as well as create a lot of black goo at the end of that tube:

- It doesn't have a proper connection.
- The sides of the tube are discharging or they're too far away.
- The pins haven't been properly cared for.

You can replace fluorescent gas tubes that are filled with rayon and mercury vapor with LED tubes. There are great substitutes nowadays, but if there aren't, then you'll need to get an old-fashioned fluorescent tube.

ALL AROUND THE CEILING FAN

There are few repairs in this book that give me a headache just thinking about them—and this is one of them! Repairing ceiling fans is notoriously tricky. I'm going to talk primarily about wobbling ceiling fans and unbalanced ceiling fans.

Disclaimer:

If a ceiling fan is violently wobbling back and forth, I don't recommend fixing it yourself. You should call in a professional because the problem could be a larger issue than just simply rebalancing the fan.

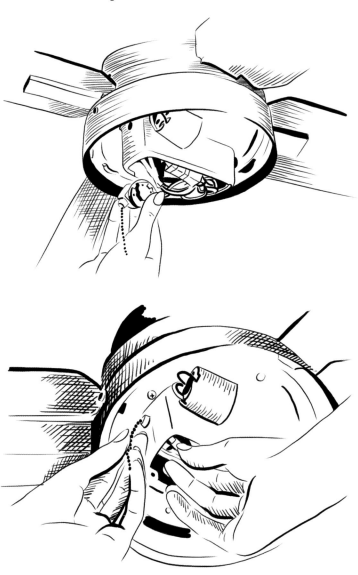

FIXING AN UNBALANCED FAN

If your ceiling fan is just making a squeaking noise, it's wobbling slightly, or the balance is a little bit out of whack, that's something you can repair—and it can be a simple fix. First, you need to diagnose the problem:

- Check the fan box or brace to ensure everything is tightened.
- Look for blade cracks, warping, or other damage.
- Clean your ceiling fan blades; sometimes excess dirt can be heavy and cause an imbalance.
- Ensure the fan blades are all at the same height.
- Use a balancing kit to make sure the blades are balanced.

If it's wobbling at the base and everything's already tightened properly, a simple repair could be putting a shim (a spacer) or something else so you can tighten the fan at the box or brace that's attached to the ceiling itself. That might be all you have to do. Sometimes, a shim doesn't look that pretty, but you often can't see it anyway or you can conceal anything that's showing. But it's a quick, easy little trick and can prevent further damage because if you allow it to continue to wobble, it can become dangerous later on.

If the blades are uneven or unbalanced and they're causing the fan to sway back and forth, you might need to get a ceiling fan balancing kit that comes with weights that are designed for ceiling fans. These kits are available at most hardware stores and online. It will come with clips and weights that have adhesive on the back to go on various portions of a fan blade. The following steps will help you use a balancing kit:

1 Clip the plastic clip to the edge of the blade—in the middle between where the fan blade is connected to the fan and the tip of the blade.

2 Turn the fan to its highest speed to see if the wobble stops or is improved. If there's no improvement, try another blade.

3 Repeat the process until you find the unbalanced blade and see some improvement from the clip placement. It doesn't need to fix the problem completely!

4 Once you find the unbalanced blade, place the clip closer to the fan base and farther away from the tip of the blade to see where it best helps balance the blade and makes the most improvement.

5 Once you've determined which blade is unbalanced and where on that blade the balance needs to occur, remove the backing of the weight and stick it on the blade in line with the clip.

6 Test the fan on its highest speed for several minutes to make sure the balance has improved.

It becomes a sort of game to tweak the balance and make it perfect, but the weight is an easy installation and I recommend it. Before you go into this project, remember that patience is key: Take your time, and make sure the weight is properly secure when you're finally done with the placement.

REPLACING A CEILING FAN PULL SWITCH

Ceiling fans often have one or two pull switches, for the light and the fan itself, which can come undone or break off. The string or chain can also break, especially if it has a ball at the end—repetitively gripping the ball can cause it to become loose. You can buy a pull switch online—it's very affordable and easy to install. But if the pull switch has come away from the base of the ceiling fan or if it's been pulled out completely, then the fan might need to be taken apart—and that's best done by a professional. But you can replace a pull switch—and the following will help you do that.

MATERIALS

wire cutters/strippers, new pull switch (three-speed or just on/off depending on your fan), and a Phillips screwdriver

1 Turn off the switch to the fan as well as the breaker associated with the fan. (See page 150 for how to turn off the breaker.)

2 Remove the screws holding the light fixture in place. Make sure you're holding the light fixture in one hand when you're removing the last screw because the fixture will drop down when released.

3 There will be a white wire tab you can press to separate and remove the base of the fixture.

4 The pull switch will typically have two wires: black and white. It might also have a ground wire. Take a picture or write down the configuration to make sure you know what's what before you begin.

"When in doubt, bail out!" If you ever feel uncomfortable, it's okay to stop the work and get help.

5 Use wire cutters to cut these wires off the switch—as close to the switch as possible. Leave about ½ inch (1.3cm) of wire exposed to attach to the new switch.

6 Attach each wire to the new switch by pushing the wire into the designated hole. Give each wire a little tug to make sure the connection is tight.

7 Remove the chain nut from the new switch, thread the chain through the hole, and attach the chain nut to the outside of the fixture.

8 Reattach and plug in the base of the fixture to the fan, put the lights back in place, and turn on the switch and breaker to test the fan and pull switch.

Emotional Reset

Electrical work can be such an overwhelming task, but as several of these showed you, not all of them are life threatening. Many of these can be something that's accessible.

But again, you look at these problems and you're happy that something works when it works and you're sad when it doesn't. And taking a moment to figure out how these processes can help you in the long run and understand how repairs are done reinforces how to troubleshoot and fix things later on.

All that's a positive influence on your knowledge base. The more you learn, the less scary these things are. Boosting your knowledge will boost your confidence in knowing you can take care of yourself and ask for the help you need. So I'm happy you read this chapter and I'm proud of you for learning as much as you can. Being prepared is never a bad thing.

12

MOLD, PESTS, AND WEATHER PREPPING

THE AWFUL ADVENTURES OF MOLD AND MILDEW

Removing mold and mildew can really improve your health. When you first start seeing any mold or mildew growing in your bathroom, shower, or bedroom, take care of it quickly before it starts to spread. Mold will start multiplying and spreading if left unchecked, and if it's black mold, you'll likely see it after it's already forming behind a wall, so it could be affecting a much larger area than you can see.

> If you do suspect black mold, please contact your landlord to get it tested before treating the area. You can likely remove a couple square feet of mold yourself with the proper protective gear and ventilation, but a larger area of black mold might require a professional remediation team.

That being said, certain products that have been advertised to remove mold effectively, such as bleach, don't actually work on mold. Bleach only gives the impression that something's being cleaned; it doesn't necessarily kill the mold spores directly.

So we're going to avoid that product altogether and focus on products with bleach-free formulas because that way, you know they're going to do their job more effectively and they're relying on facts, not myths, for their claims.

- Buy a mold-killing spray of some kind (that has no bleach in it) and spray it on the surface area.
- Spray a larger area than what you can see. If the area of mold looks a few inches wide, I want you to go wider—and even beyond that—because the mold spores are probably reaching beyond what's visible. So for a few inches of mold, spray at least a foot around the area.
- Once you apply the spray, follow the directions on the spray bottle. Most of them will want you to wait anywhere between 15 and 20 minutes before removing the spray.
- Once the spray has soaked in and you've waited the required time, use a mixture of vinegar and water to wipe the area you sprayed. Vinegar will help neutralize the mold and mildew and will keep them from coming back and getting much worse.
- Use soap and water to clean off any residue left behind.

Do this routine twice a week for about 2 or 3 weeks or for however long the problem persists. Even when you can't see mold growing, it's still there. This will help kill any remnants that aren't visible to the naked eye.

The next thing that you want to do is address the root of the problem, which is typically caused by dampness in the air. If you have poor ventilation in your home or if you don't have any fans in your bathroom, this will cause moisture to accumulate, which is how mold and mildew grow. Taking care of ventilation will make sure this problem doesn't happen again.

Using a dehumidifier, even a small one, will go a long way toward helping prevent the growth of mold and mildew.

- For safety reasons, don't run the dehumidifier when you're not home because dehumidifiers can be dangerous if they don't have an automatic shutoff when they're full. Because of this, invest in a dehumidifier that turns off after a certain time, when it tips over, or when it's full. This protects your home from flooding and from water damage if anything happens while you're away.

- A dehumidifier will help prevent the further growth of mold. It can even help kill the mold or mildew because removing the moisture in the area will destroy their ability to grow because that's what they thrive on.

- If the mold problem is in a bathroom area, remember that moisture is going to naturally happen in there no matter what you do. So running a fan or dehumidifier 20 minutes before a hot shower and 20 to 30 minutes after is ideal. This will help make sure the area is nice and dry before and fairly dry afterward.

- If you see any water collecting on top of the ceiling or on the walls, that means the moisture and heat in the room are too hot for the ventilation system. The ventilation should prevent any water droplets from accumulating in those areas. If the water droplets are accumulating in those areas, that means you have poor ventilation for how hot that water is and you need to make sure you remedy that to reduce the potential for mold to grow.

THE NEVER–JUST–RIGHT FORECAST (WEATHER-PROTECTING YOUR HOME)

Protecting a home and keeping a home safe are very much related to the weatherization of your home, regardless of whether it's winter or a hot summer. Take precautions to keep your home safe inside and outside for all who live there.

If you're in a place that doesn't normally freeze or your pipes aren't insulated when installed, you'll want to leave the water dripping from each faucet in the house. A light drip with one to two drops of water at a time is sufficient to keep the water moving so it doesn't freeze. If the pipes do freeze, open the faucet for the pipe(s) that is/are frozen and use a hair dryer or another heat source to slowly heat the pipes. Don't bang or hit frozen pipes.

WINTER WEATHERIZATION

Weatherization for winter isn't just about cost. It's also about how to keep your home warm and make sure you're safe. Here are some easy tips for getting started:

- **Window film:** This plastic covering will seal your windows and prevent drafts.

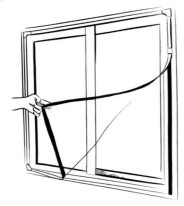

- **Curtains:** Thick thermal curtains that are dark can insulate and trap heat.
- **Latex caulk:** This seals any openings at joints, seams, or cracks.
- **Weather stripping:** Helps to seal air leaks in areas of your home, such as doors, windows, and attics. This can include vinyl, felt, tape, or door sweeps.
- **Air conditioner protection:** Clean the area around the AC unit and place a piece of plywood over the outdoor unit. Make sure to remove ice and snow often so it doesn't accumulate. Don't cover your AC unit with plastic because this can trap moisture inside and attract small animals.

- **Draft stoppers:** A draft stopper (also called a draft blocker) is a snake-like cloth tube stuffed with batting, rice, beans, or other material. Laid across cracks under doors and around windows, a draft stopper acts like fabric weather stripping.

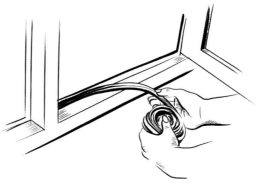

- **Space heaters:** Make sure to get the kind that shut off if they're tipped over.
- **Faucet insulation cover:** This attaches to the exterior of a house and covers the hose spigot with an insulated cover to prevent freezing on outdoor faucets.

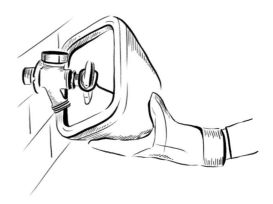

SUMMER WEATHERIZATION

In the summer, it's also important to apply a lot of the same tactics to keep your cool air inside the home:

- Weather-strip and caulk all seams, joints, and cracks.
- Use blackout curtains that have a white exterior-facing side to reflect heat.
- A dehumidifier can help remove moisture from the air and keep mold and mildew from growing in the damp heat.
- If you don't have air conditioning, you can use a box fan in your window. Place it facing toward the exterior in one room and open a window in another. This will create suction and a breeze in your home.

STOP BUGGING ME!

We've reached the section that terrifies me the most—and that's pests! As a maintenance technician, I constantly receive questions about pests. And there isn't always a great answer. I want to be able to have an answer that can fix all the pest problems—from bedbugs, cockroaches, and flies to rodents and birds.

Let's start with the basics and things you can be aware of, like how pests can get into your home or what attracts them to your home:

- Cracks that aren't sealed
- Spots where pipes enter the home in the bathroom, kitchen, or basement
- Windows and doors not properly sealed
- Doors being left open
- Foundations that aren't sealed
- Coming in with you on your clothing

- Secondhand furniture or clothing
- Packages that were left outside
- Food left out and not cleaned up
- Pet food on the floor
- Large amounts of clutter
- Even a neighbor who has these issues that go undetected

Luckily, there are ways to prevent these pests from entering your home!

- Make sure to clean secondhand clothing and furniture properly. Using Lysol spray or a vinegar spray when bringing things into your home can prevent things like bedbugs.
- Clean the bottoms of your shoes often with Lysol or vinegar.
- Occasionally take a look around your home for the entrances that rodents can get into. You can place pet-safe traps at these entrances or close them up for good.
- Invest in screens for your windows or doors so when they're open, pests can't get inside.
- Clean up all food as soon as possible, take out the trash regularly, and keep your pet food bowls clean by washing them regularly.
- Keep roach and ant baits on hand, but only put them out if you see these pests around the house.
- Use a garment steamer to clean linens, curtains, furniture, and mattresses for bedbugs.
- Powders, such as diatomaceous earth, spread at entrances or areas that are infested can help kill small pests, like cockroaches, because it damages their exoskeleton.

When it comes to ants, cockroaches, flies, etc., there are various products that can kill these critters. But it's important to know you might not be the source of these pests. You now know what you can do to reduce opportunities for these pests to get into your home, but when you're living in an apartment building, there's a chance one person isn't upholding their end of the bargain and they might be the prime source. You might have the cleanest apartment and you might have the most pristine home, but that won't matter if someone else in that apartment building isn't being mindful of what they're bringing into the complex. Even new apartment buildings aren't immune to this problem.

Contact your landlord as soon as possible when dealing with pests. In most states, it's the landlord's responsibility to call pest control and remedy the issue. As long as you're doing your part to keep your home clean, the landlord should comply with supplying pest control. As always, make sure to document any issues, get everything in writing, and take note of all the strategies you're using to control the pests within your home.

There's so much information about pests that it's hard to go into great detail with every single aspect of this. Honestly, one could write a whole book just on pests themselves! I will say, though, that while pest control can be overwhelming and there might not be black-and-white solutions, do the best you can with reducing the likelihood of getting them inside your home and make sure you feel safe in your home. Just know that you're doing an amazing job and hopefully that will give you some solace.

Emotional Reset

Whether you're dealing with weather-related issues, pests, or even black mold or mildew, it's important you don't overlook these things. They can end up creating a much larger issue for you. There isn't always a clear-cut solution to these problems—and that's okay. Sometimes, we have to understand there are limitations to what we can do. Not only as renters but also as humans. It can be hard to fix an entire black mold issue without replacing the entire affected area. It can be hard to deal with cockroaches and pests without dealing with the whole building. And it can be hard to make sure you weatherize your home without proper insulation. So keep in mind you can do the best you can do with all the information in this chapter, but if you don't achieve it perfectly, it doesn't mean you failed.

Attempting these things, learning from them, and doing the best you can are more than enough. I'm proud of you for attempting to learn this and I'm proud of you for not getting discouraged by these situations. Know that if a pest comes back, if mold starts growing again, if something goes wrong during winter, it doesn't mean you failed. It means the system we live in failed you and your home wasn't set up for you to succeed. But you're doing the best you can with what you have—and I'm proud of you for that. And I'm proud of you for making your house or apartment your home despite things you can't control. You're doing a great job!

APPLIANCE
REPAIRS AND
UPKEEP

THE ICEBOX INVESTIGATION: COMMON FRIDGE AND FREEZER TROUBLESHOOTING

As with all the appliance sections, I don't want to send you down a path that's going to get you into trouble, but I'm going to talk about common fridge and freezer problems and troubleshooting solutions so you can diagnose a problem or even fix small problems in some cases.

Whenever you're having any problems with your fridge and/or freezer, you want to use this checklist first:

* When you open up the door to your refrigerator, the light should come on. If the light's not coming on, that means you might not have power to the fridge, or the bulb may need to be replaced. These are typically 40W appliance bulbs—simply remove the existing bulb and take it to the store for a replacment. If the light is coming on, that means you have power and the fridge is plugged in.

* Check if the thermostat is at the same temperature it usually is. Sometimes, it gets bumped and even just 1 or 2 notches on your typical refrigerator can make a huge difference in temperature.

* There are vents on the inside of your fridge and at the back. If these vents are blocked in any way, that can prevent the proper flow of air. One of the most common things I'll see is people will overpack the fridge and that will cause a problem with ventilation.

* The same thing can happen with freezers. Freezers will also have vents on the inside and in back, and if those are blocked, ice can build up. It's okay if the freezer's a little bit full—just be aware that that could be causing a problem. Make sure you regularly move things around in the freezer.

- If you can pull the fridge away from the wall (check to make sure there aren't any restrictions about this in your lease), you should be cleaning behind the fridge every six months at least. You want to make sure you're not having a buildup of dust, dirt, or even random things that fall behind the fridge.

- If you can't get to the back to clean it, even getting a can of condensed air and blowing from the front underneath the fridge will do a lot to keep it away from the coils. What you don't want to happen is have dust and debris choke up your condenser. Your condenser is what helps keep the whole thing cool. If airflow can't go through, that's going to put more strain on the condenser, which is going to burn it out.

- If your freezer is full of ice, foam, etc., and if it's making its own little snow event, you might need to defrost the whole fridge and freezer by unplugging it and leaving the doors open. Make sure to transfer everything to a safe cooler or ask a friend to store your items for you. It might take about a day or two to fully defrost and melt all the ice that's built up. You can sometimes help it along with a blow dryer or large fan pointed at the ice. Once a year is what you need to do for older refrigerators. Often, though, this isn't a common occurrence as much anymore because appliances have gotten more and more advanced over the years. But every once in a while, you'll still encounter a fridge that needs some defrosting.

- If your fridge dispenses water or has an ice maker, there's most likely a filter. Make sure to look up your fridge model to find the best filter for you. If the filter isn't replaced regularly, it can build up over time and cause the system to stop making ice or dispensing water. These can sometimes be expensive, so ask your landlord or technician for a replacement and set a reminder on your calendar to replace it in the recommended amount of time, usually three to six months, so you can put in another work order for one. (Check your lease to make sure you're not responsible for these. If it's not mentioned, then it's usually on the landlord to buy the filter.)

If your issues seem to be beyond basic ventilation, maintenance, and cleaning, that's when you need to call an appliance technician or call your landlord and they'll see what they can do about this problem. But checking all this before you call is always great because then you know more before you ask for help.

REVERSING THE FRIDGE DOOR AND HANDLE

There are times when the fridge you're given in an apartment doesn't make sense—the handles might seem misaligned or the door swings the wrong way. But you can actually switch this around fairly easily for most models. This works best for models that have a freezer on top and a fridge door on the bottom.

MATERIALS

Phillips screwdriver, Allen key, and a drill

1 Remove all food from the fridge and freezer.

2 Remove any plastic covers and caps on both sides of the fridge and for the freezer and fridge doors. These cover the holes where you'll be moving the screws to. Place them in a bag and label them to help you keep track of where each cover goes when you're done.

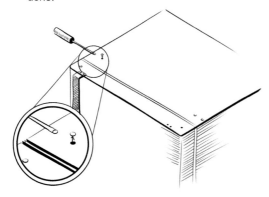

3 Start taking out the screws of the mounting bracket for the freezer door. This will be with a Philips or an Allen key of some kind, usually ⁵⁄₁₆. If the bracket has been there for a long time, it might be a little hard to remove these screws, so if you can't get them, don't force them.

4 Remove the bottom brace, take the door off, and move the bracket and brace to the other side. You're going to need to move fairly quickly because the freezer is still plugged in and running.

5 Repeat the removal process for the fridge door, removing the mounting bracket and bottom brace. Because the fridge door is usually much larger, before you take each bracket off, make sure to support the door and remove the tension on it so it's a little bit easier to lift.

6 If there's a mounting plate that's on the door, you'll need to remove that and put it on the other side of the door. It will usually be on the bottom.

7 When you put the bracket and brace on the other side, start by screwing the screws in by hand to hopefully prevent some stripping and then you can use a drill to screw them in the rest of the way.

8 Once all the brackets and braces have been moved to the other side, you're going to put all the caps you took off and put them on the other side. You're just filling the holes with the caps for the holes for the screws that were removed to take the braces and mounts off.

If you have the type of fridge that has a handle (or two handles—one for the freezer and one for the fridge)—moving it is the same basic concept as switching a bracket or brace: Unscrew the screws for the handle. Remove the screw that's inside of the freezer, screw the handle to the other side, and insert the plugs on the other side.

These swaps always look a little bit harder if you haven't seen them done, but once you try these switches yourself, you'll see that the instructions all make sense.

THE LITTLE OVEN THAT COULDN'T

Because of the nature of working with gas, I'm going to focus on electric ovens only. For gas ovens, please see your oven manual and contact your maintenance technician right away. If you ever suspect a leak, don't hesitate to call the fire department, which can help you turn off your gas and check for leaks.

HEATING ELEMENT

The most common issue with an oven is the heating element. It's the long tube that gets red when the oven is on and working, and it's the source of heat. I don't recommend trying to replace it yourself if you're not familiar with ovens, but having some knowledge of how it works can help you diagnose the issue and communicate with your landlord or maintenance technician.

The heating element is in the base of an electric oven, on the bottom below the racks. And the middle part—the part that curves inward—should be red hot when it's on. If it's not, then the element needs to be replaced.

There will also be visible breaks on the element that could often lead to it not working. You might even see a blister or two on it. These are just like round blisters that are visible on the element themselves.

If the oven typically has a light and you open it up and there's no light, it might have lost power to the electrical box or the oven itself and that might be something you also want to think about.

You might have a loose wire or a wire that's broken in the heating element itself. Yes, you can unscrew the heating element from the back of the oven and then take a look at it. I'd unplug the oven whenever you're working with the element and turn off the oven breakers to make sure you're safe and just take a look at it. You don't need to do all this work to replace the heating element if you don't want to or you're not comfortable, but just knowing that the wire's loose or something's busted on it can help you indicate to a repair technician what to do. It's common for it to be burnt out by the heating source or by where those wires connect with the element.

So don't freak out if you see any burning or glowing. That's common and nothing to be scared of—it's just a natural occurrence that can be replaced.

STOVE BURNERS

If you have a burner on top of the stove that goes out, it might have some type of connection that's wrong or the part that connects the burner to the heating element inside on the top of the oven has gone bad. Check to make sure that everything connected is good and there are no charred unwires or anything like that.

If you have a stove that isn't a glass top and has burners and burner plates, those burner plates under the burner need to be replaced regularly or when they're very dirty. You can remove all the pieces and clean them thoroughly, but if there's a lot of buildup that isn't coming off, that can be a fire hazard.

A lot of times, people like to get black ones so you don't see as much grease and stuff—and that's all fine and dandy. But the way these are designed, the silver ones showcase the dirt and charring so you know when to replace them. The black ones can sometimes hide that, but grease buildup isn't good for your burners.

People often put aluminum foil around these burner plates and it's not safe to do that because that can actually lead to a grease fire. The same thing can happen if you put aluminum foil underneath the oven door itself. That can be a hazard and I don't recommend it. If you want to catch the grease and food, use an oven mat that's made to go below the heating element. But in this instance, cleaning it after you're done is the best route to prevent grease buildup rather than trying to collect it.

THE VERY HUNGRY GARBAGE DISPOSAL

Fixing garbage disposals is one of the most common repairs I did over my 14-year career as a technician. It seemed like every day, I was clearing debris, resetting the disposal, or replacing one of these so-called "magical go-away machines."

But it's very important to remember that these are in fact NOT "magical go-away machines." There are certain things we should avoid putting into a garbage disposal, such as eggshells, potato skins, and grease. Running the water before you begin, turning on the disposal, and then gradually putting into the disposal what you'd like to chop up will significantly help avoid problems altogether. Loading up your disposal and then turning it on will cause it to overheat and flip its internal breaker.

Never **EVER** stick your fingers or anything breakable down the garbage disposal while it's running. This could lead to injury or even damage to the unit.

REPAIRING A GARBAGE DISPOSAL

If you run the disposal and there's no noise being made, then you might just have a flipped internal fuse. The internal fuse prevents damage to the equipment and keeps the garbage disposal from catching fire.

If you run the disposal and you hear a buzzing noise, you might have one of two problems:

- Something is lodged inside the disposal.

- The motor is burnt out and you might need a new disposal.

With the unit unplugged (or the associated circuit breaker turned off), use a flashlight and peer into the unit to see if there's a visible problem. Look toward the sides. Something as small as an earring can get lodged inside and prevent the unit from spinning. If there's water standing in the unit and you can't see anything, don't you worry. You can deal with this in the following steps.

MATERIALS

flashlight, ¼ Allen key, needle-nose pliers, tongs, and a claw tool

1 Make sure to unplug the unit or turn off the associated circuit breaker.

2 Go under the sink and reset the unit. You'll see a red reset button on the underside of the disposal. If it's pushed out, just push it back in.

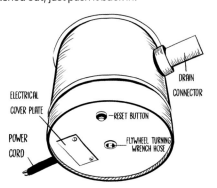

ELECTRICAL COVER PLATE

POWER CORD

—RESET BUTTON

FLYWHEEL TURNING WRENCH HOSE

DRAIN CONNECTOR

HOW DO YOU KNOW IF IT WORKED?

- Fill a small tub, bucket, or bowl with no more than 20 ice cubes, a little dish soap, and some water. Turn on the water again and then run your disposal.

- Gradually pour the contents of the bowl down the drain. Not only will this test the unit, but it will also help clean your unit. Don't shove ice cubes down there and then turn on the unit. That will likely flip the breaker or damage the machine.

- If the unit gets flipped, chances are your disposal will need to be replaced soon and it's time to call your maintenance tech.

3 If the reset button wasn't sticking out, then you might have a burnt-out motor or something lodged in the unit. Proceed with the following steps regardless of what you find to make sure you correctly fix the problem.

4 Under the unit will also be a place for you to put a ¼ Allen key. (This is the standard size, but it might vary). Place the Allen key in the slot and rotate it back and forth. If you think of it as a clock and you're starting at 3 p.m., rotate the key back and forth to 6 p.m. and 12 p.m. several times. This helps to dislodge anything that might be stuck and can also clear standing water that might still be inside the unit.

5 With the unit still off, look inside the disposal. This time, there should be no water and any lodged objects should be more clearly visible.

6 Use needle-nose pliers, a claw tool, or tongs to remove any objects remaining inside the machine.

7 Plug the unit back in and flip the circuit breaker back on. Run water down the drain and then turn on the disposal. Let it run for at least 1 minute to flush out any remaining debris.

THE WONDERFUL WASHER OF DISHES

The following are tips and tricks that might help you with your dishwasher. Some of these might sound familiar or might be completely new to you.

- There will be prongs inside of the top shelf of your dishwasher. The prongs are actually meant for your mugs and your wine glasses. They'll help make sure these containers are at an angle and upside down so they don't collect water.

- And if you're thinking "Mercury, my wine glasses are too tall to go on the top shelf of my dishwasher!"—that would be true, but the top rack of the dishwasher was designed for wine glasses. So you can put them at an angle, laying them down at 45°.

- You can actually drop down your top dishwasher shelf by pushing in two levers. If your dishwasher doesn't have that, it likely has tabs on the end of the drawer tracks you can push to remove the top drawer completely. This will allow you to fit much larger things in the bottom of your dishwasher for cleaning.

- You don't have to rinse your dishes off prior to washing. Just make sure to remove any bits of food that are bigger than a grain of rice by scraping them into your trash or compost. Your dishwasher detergent actually needs something to adhere to to clean the dishes, so your dishes will get cleaner if you leave some residue on them.

- It's proven you can use a lot less water by running the dishwasher every night—even if it's not full. You don't actually use that much water in your dishwasher. It's a misconception that people think it saves water to hand wash, but it doesn't.

- Your dishes should always be placed toward the center so they're facing inward rather than facing outward. That will help get the blast of water they need from the water sprayer below.

- There's also the spinning sprayer that's underneath the top shelf. Make sure nothing is hitting that sprayer. That sprayer is going to release water and that's good—you want that—but if something is blocking the sprayer, like a larger pan or a larger dish, that's going to prevent the sprayer from spinning and then prevent the dishes on the top rack from getting clean.

- Here's one of my favorite hacks I've seen on TikTok. A lot of times, the dishes will still be a little bit damp and steamy after they're done being cleaned. Instead of just letting them sit in there and dry out for a long time, you can actually open the dishwasher door, hang a towel on the door so it's half in and half out, then gently rest the door closed. Just make sure not to push it completely shut so you don't damage the locking mechanism. If you'd prefer, you can also place the whole towel inside so it doesn't interfere with the locking mechanism when shutting the door. All that moisture is then going to get sucked into the cloth and it's going to make it all dry in there. It only takes 5 minutes and it works pretty well.

- Dishwasher pods should go in the detergent slot, contrary to what some people advise. If you have issues with the pod sticking and not being released, try these two things: Make sure your hands are completely dry before touching the pod and wipe out the detergent slot with a towel to make sure it's also dry. This will prevent sticking but also save your pod during the pre-rinse cycle so the machine has all the soap it needs during the main wash cycle.

- If you have a stinky dishwasher, you can add vinegar to the bottom and run an empty cycle. This will help with the smell. Sometimes, that vinegar is just so good at breaking down old odors and neutralizing things. Use maybe 2 or 3 tablespoons—nothing much. If you need to use 1 cup or ½ cup, that's usually also okay.

- Make sure to also clean the filters in your dishwasher. Below the sprayer on the bottom of your dishwasher is a piece that looks like a filter or a cup. There's also a guard around it. You can take all those pieces off and wash them in the sink with soap and water. If there's a clog, check the holes under this filter to make sure they're clear. There's one more filter on the door of the dishwasher, usually on the upper left of the inside of the door. Pop that out to also give it a clean. These might be things you want to clean when you first get into your new rental or if you have a clog.

- Don't ever use regular dish soap in your dishwasher. It can cause a lot of foaming and it can actually create leaks inside your dishwasher as well as cause one heck of a flood.

- It's best to have all your utensils pointed up, like spoons, forks, and butter knives. For safety, you should put any sharp knives down. This will help the utensils get cleaner because they'll be more exposed to the water and soap this way.

- Make sure there's nothing parallel against the door itself. If you have something like a cookie sheet or baking pan that's going to be up against the door, it might not actually dispense the detergent and that's not going to be good.

- If you have any clogs in your dishwasher, treat that like you would if you had a clog in a sink or tub. Under the sink, find where the dishwasher line is connected to your main line, usually just above the P-trap. It should look like a small hose. Usually, you'll only need a flathead screwdriver to remove the metal band around the hose and release it. You can use your hands or your screwdriver to remove any debris at the end of the hose and then shake it out to try to get any debris out. Also do this same thing to the part of the line attached to your main pipe. Place everything back as it was once when you're done.

- If your dishwasher has a spot for a rinse aid, use it! It's essentially required these days if your dishwasher was made for it to get your dishes fully cleaned. If you don't use it, you might notice you always have wet dishes—even after a heated dry cycle. Water sitting on your dishes and not getting completely dried during the cycle is what causes water spots.

THE GIVING UNIT: AIR CONDITIONER REPAIRS

While I don't recommend making major repairs on your appliances, there are some common problems and issues you can learn about to help you keep your appliances working properly. One of the problems you might have is an air conditioner that's no longer producing the same amount of cold air or it takes a lot longer to cool off the space. If you've lived there for a few years or even just a few months and you notice a big difference, it could be that one of your filters is clogged or dirty.

If you have central air and heat, you'll have two to three different types of filters or screens:

- Intake filter
- HVAC or furnace filter
- AC unit screen

Handy Ma'am Tip:

Check your lease to make sure you're not responsible for replacing filters. If it's not mentioned in your lease at all, then it's usually the responsibility of the landlord.

INTAKE OR RETURN FILTERS

The intake filter is likely behind a grate somewhere in a ceiling or a wall. These filters are more common in duplexes, townhouses, or houses than in apartments, where they're less common. This is where the air is pulled from inside your house to the AC unit to cool off the dwelling, which is usually why they're up high, as warm air rises. They vary in size, but if you open the grate, it will reveal a cardboard-framed filter. This frame will have the size written on it and will show you in which direction to put the filter back when you're replacing it.

These should be replaced every few months and you can often get a subscription that will automatically mail them to you every three months. If you live in an area that has a lot of trees/pollen, pets, etc., you might need to replace it more often. Once you replace yours, check back after two weeks to see how it's doing. If it's already full, then there might be an issue with your unit or the home itself for it to be getting dirty so quickly. The filters are fairly cheap, so you can get them yourself or ask your landlord or technician if you're comfortable.

FURNACE FILTERS

There might also be HVAC or furnace filters that are in the part of the unit that's inside your home, usually behind a closet or in the attic. This is most common if your heating system is the same as your AC system. You likely won't have one if you have a boiler or radiator-style heating system. I'd double check with your lease and/or landlord before changing the furnace filter because some landlords would prefer to do this themselves. I share this information just in case you find yourself in a situation where your furnace filter isn't being changed regularly and you'd like to make sure you've got it squared away.

These will also be the cardboard-framed filters, with all the information found on the frame. The filter itself is usually on top of or below the main part of the furnace and you'll replace it similarly to a return air filter. These should also be replaced every three to four months, ideally before a change in weather from hot to cold or cold to hot. I recommend running your furnace after changing the filter to make sure everything is working properly.

Some furnace filters might be permanent or metal filters, although this is less common. Permanent filters can either be taken outside and blown out with an air compressor can or washed in a sink or tub. Even an old toothbrush and just scrubbing all the stuff off it or vacuuming up the dust will be all you need to do. Let it dry and then put it back in.

You can also get replacements for these if they crack or are broken or if there are a whole bunch of holes and a lot of that debris is getting stuck in the coils of the air conditioner. So if you just replace it with a new filter, that will also do the trick. If you type in "air conditioning filter" on Google or even go to a hardware store, you'll usually find a screen that will work, but getting it to be the right shape is the tricky part. If you can bring the old piece with you, bring the measurements, or take a picture of it, that will help you. You can also get the HVAC model number and look up the filter that way. Just keep in mind these can be a bit more expensive— between $50–100—so talk to your landlord or maintenance technician if you can.

A/C UNIT SCREEN

If you're able to access the air conditioner from outside, then you can also clean that. Make sure all the vents on the side of the air conditioner are free from debris. That's going to make it run a little better. It's sucking the air in from those

vents and then pushing it out. It's essentially what it does—that's how it makes everything cold inside your home. So you need those vents open for them to do their best job.

Sometimes, you'll see beehives on them or you'll see birds have built nests on them because they can be hot outside and it's metal and it can keep their eggs warm when they're not on it. All this can lead to problems. So if you see anything building or forming, keep an eye on it. You can either hose it off or vacuum it if you can. You can also take the protector screen off and clean the sides.

If you can't remove the outer screen or none of these steps have helped your AC start to cool you off better, then this is where you'd ask for help from your landlord or technician. There are tons of tutorials that will show you how to take everything apart online and just show you how to put it all back together. Out of caution, I won't be going into that here because if anything goes wrong, that can cause issues, but you can try if you're brave enough to take things apart, clean all the parts and make sure they dry out. I'd recommend taking a photo of each step along the way. Taking a photo before you do each step or even a video of you taking it all apart will save you down the line—and I highly recommend doing this if possible.

WINDOW UNITS

Window units are less complicated but still have filters. These are most likely permanent rather than disposal, though, and are a screen behind a grate. You can usually pop open the grate to reveal the screen. Most of these are removable but might not. Use a paper towel, dry toothbrush, or dry rag or cloth to clean it off. If you can remove it, you can wash it. Wait until it's completely dry, then replace it. You can also clean around the filter and the grate with a damp cloth while you have the screen open or out. I also recommend going outside if you're on the ground floor or have a balcony and wiping down the exterior side of the unit.

All this being said, your landlord should be cleaning out any AC unit or furnace and providing routine maintenance and cleaning from a professional or technician at least once a year. Ask your technician the last time your unit was cleaned and mark your calendars for one year from then to remind you to place a work order for that routine cleaning.

But replacing filters, checking all the vents, cleaning what you can, etc., will likely save your problem. Doing this regularly as preventative care will ensure your air conditioner will be able to do its job for a long time.

THE WHIRLY TWIRLY WASHER AND DRYER

I want to remind you that if you're a renter and you don't have a washer and dryer or a dishwasher or any of the other appliances mentioned in this chapter, that's okay. Maybe you will in your next home. But I want to make sure you have the knowledge to know how to make repairs to them if you can. So let's look at some ways to handle everyday issues with your washer and dryer.

WASHING MACHINES

Most washers now are high-efficiency washers, which means they don't need as much water and they also don't need as much detergent. You want to make sure that if it says high efficiency, or HE, you don't need more than 2 tablespoons of detergent. Any more than that can cause some severe problems, such as leaving residue, preventing your clothes from getting clean, creating buildup in your washer, or making things overly smelly. Less is more—you don't need a ton of detergent to clean your clothes.

I always advise people to not overload their washer, to not try to put everything in there, and to not pack down all their clothes. Small to medium loads are actually better. Your clothes don't actually get clean from the soap and water. They get cleaned from friction—either your clothes rubbing together as they tumble or from an agitator in the middle. The soap helps the water rinse it all away, but it's the friction you need.

Overloading your washer will mean less friction and thus less clean clothes. Doing a smaller load is going to get your laundry cleaner and you don't use as much water for washers as you think you do—and that's also a big part of this process.

TYPES OF WASHING MACHINES

- **Front-load:** Reducing the load of a front-load washer is especially important! These don't have agitators in the middle and rely on the tumbling of the clothes around the washer to create the friction they need to get the clothes clean. There needs to be enough space in the washing machine for the clothes to tumble and get enough friction.

- **Top-load with an agitator:** If you have a top-load washer, make sure you wrap your clothes around the agitator rather than placing them on the top. If you place things on the top or overfill the washer, then the agitator can't grab the clothes and move them around, so they're not going to get wet and there won't be enough friction to get them clean.
- **Top-load without an agitator:** If you have a washer that doesn't have the agitator in the middle, then you should still load the washer like it's a donut rather than just throwing everything into the middle. It probably even says this in the manual for the washer, but you want to load it like a donut, keeping the center open so it can actually have room to clean your stuff inside of it. Again, it's that friction I keep talking about.

Essentially, be sure not to overload your washer. It can cause a lot of different problems if you don't. You'll notice that your machine is moving too much when spinning, making loud clanking noises, or not fully spinning and your clothes come out dripping wet still. If this happens often enough, then you can throw your washer out of balance or even break parts inside the washer! But if you load your clothes properly, you'll keep the washer running smoothly for many years to come.

Handy Ma'am Tip:

I recommend reading instruction manuals when you move into a new apartment. Look up the manual for the make and model of your washer and dryer because that can make a big difference. You can find any manual online these days. Washers also often have loading instructions on the lids. These will teach you how to use the washer properly so you can keep it safe and running smoothly for a long time.

DRYERS

When it comes to your dryer, here are some things to keep you safe and to help you dry your clothes more efficiently:

- Make sure the lint collector is doing its job well. Always clean it out, and when you remove the lint catcher, it's always best to take a stripper or some type of a brush to remove the rest of the lint that might have gotten stuck down in that space. It's good to also make sure you can get a vacuum hose down it and suck as much of the lint out as possible.
- Regularly clean the lint from the dryer hose. It will be a shiny silver tube coming out of the back of your dryer that runs to a vent that goes outside. If this gets clogged—as it does over time—it will prevent your clothes from drying because all the moisture will be trapped inside. This can also cause a fire hazard if the moisture can't escape and continues to get too hot because your dryer is compensating for the lack of ventilation.

Handy Ma'am Reminder:

Remember, this might not be possible if you're a renter. You might not have access to clean your dryer hose—and that's okay. Place a work order for regular maintenance when you move in and then at least once a year or more often if you have a large family and do a lot of laundry.

- Another issue to be aware of with the dryer hose is looking for any kinks in the hose that are preventing air flow or if the hose is going straight up and out, like if it's in a basement. While you can remove any kinks in the hose, you might not be able to change the placement of it. Just make sure to occasionally remove the end that's attached to the dryer and shake any lint or debris out that's sinking to the bottom of the hose and not venting outside.

- If you can, I also recommend going outside and finding where the vent is on the outside of the building. Make sure it has a grate on it so no debris can fall into it from outside and make sure that grate is clear of any debris, such as leaves or lint. If you live on a second floor or higher, take a look outside to see from the ground or balcony. You can use your phone camera to zoom in to see more clearly. This way, you can diagnose if there's an issue and put a work order in ASAP.

- If your dryer has a sensor dry option, keep in mind these are only good for smaller loads that don't have mixed fabrics. If you have something like a towel that takes a long time to dry and a bunch of cotton T-shirts that dry quickly, the sensor won't be able to properly detect if the whole load is dry or not. The same is true if the load is too large. I recommend using a timed dry option for anything that isn't a small load and has the same type of clothing.

- The sensor can also get dirty if you use dryer sheets or overuse detergent in your washer. Dryer sheets can coat everything with a waxy substance and aren't recommended by professionals. They look like one or two curved metal bars just inside the dryer next to the link trap. Take a wet rag or cloth and a drop of mild soap and wipe the sensor bars clean. Then wipe them dry and make sure they're completely dry before you run another load.

Handy Ma'am Tip:

Use wool balls instead of dryer sheets. They're cheap, work better, are reusable, and don't leave residue.

- Something that can also happen is the heating element can go bad. The heating element can be fairly easily replaced, but it's a job for a professional. So if you've checked that everything is clean and clear and your dryer still isn't working properly, you know it's now time to ask for help.

These are all the things you can do when it comes to trying to fix the heat of your dryer. For years, even with the help of professionals, my dryer has always been a little bit slower. Just do smaller loads and make sure you've done all the tricks and tips here.

But I understand how frustrating that can be, but truthfully, you can only do as good of a job as the equipment you have can do—and that's okay.

Emotional Reset

If you've read it through this chapter and there are parts that don't apply to you because maybe you don't have a washer and dryer in your unit or maybe you don't have a dishwasher, that's okay. It's okay that you don't have these things in your home. I know it can be overwhelming sometimes when you read these things and they don't apply to you. Maybe you have a small home. Maybe you live in a big city where you only have 200-300 square feet in your home or less. It can be overwhelming to see these things that other people have, knowing you don't have these. And I want to just reassure you again that it's okay—that you're not less valuable and you're not less valid.

There've been many moments in my life where I think I'm moving forward, but in fact, I'm not. I feel like I'm moving sideways or backward—and that can be difficult. I need to remind you that I was homeless for five months several years back before I transitioned—and it was hard for me. I didn't have many things. I'd watch home repair videos because it was my job and I had to learn how to help people who had more than me—and it was difficult. I'd constantly be reminded of not having much. But I'd remind myself every single day that someone else's possessions weren't my shortcoming. That just because someone else had things I didn't doesn't mean I was a bad person. It doesn't mean I was a failure and it doesn't mean I'm lesser.

Knowing that—and learning to be okay with that—has helped me a lot. I want you to also be okay with that. And on the flip side, if you're someone who for the first time in your life has these things and now it's overwhelming because they don't seem to always work, that's okay. My best advice is to always try to rely on the information that's out there. Appliances will typically have a hotline you can call or you look up the manual of your make and model online.

There are little things you can accidentally gloss over when you have these things that can be crucial in maintaining them because they're like us: They're all different and they all have different purposes and different styles, so don't make any assumptions about what you know and always be willing to learn. And even if you miss something and make a mistake, that's also okay. That doesn't mean you're less than. You learn at different times and I'm proud of you for doing what you can. But that's what it's all about: doing what you can when you can with what you have. I'm proud of you. You have more than you realize.

SECURITY
AND SAFETY

GO BAGS FOR EMERGENCIES

There are many things that we can't account for. Fire from excess heat, flooding damage, storms, tornadoes, and hurricanes are all great examples. Understand that all these natural disasters that occur can be unexpected, but you can prepare a go bag for emergencies that will help you with whatever might come.

Your go bag should include:

- Water
- Nonperishable foods
- Battery-powered or hand-crank radio
- Flashlight
- First-aid kit
- Batteries
- Whistle
- Dust mask
- Plastic sheeting
- Duct tape
- Wet wipes
- Wrench or pliers
- Can opener
- Maps
- Cell phone chargers and battery packs

SMOKE DETECTORS

When it comes to security and safety in your home, you might overlook smoke detectors and CO_2 detectors. You need to regularly make sure they're properly connected and tested, which includes ensuring the batteries are working.

I always like to make sure I have a stash of 9-volt batteries as well as AA and AAA batteries because these are the most common ones that are used with smoke and CO_2 detectors. Make sure to test smoke detector batteries every month by pressing the test button. If your detectors use regular batteries, replace them at least once a year.

1   Use a ladder or step stool to reach the detector.

2   Twist the cover for the detector a quarter turn counterclockwise.

3   There will be either a visible battery once the cover has been removed or there will be a small lever to open the place where the battery is.

4   Replace the old battery with the correct new battery, making sure to place the positive end on the positive side (+) and the negative end on the negative side (−).

5   Return the cover to its proper place and give it a quarter turn clockwise until it clicks into place.

Because alarm sensors wear out, the detector should also be replaced at least every 10 years.

The date of manufacture for your alarm is printed in date format on the back of the detector. If it's more than 10 years old, contact maintenance or your landlord for a new one.

Smoke detectors can be such an annoying thing when they start beeping at you, but that's not a bad thing. When you hear beeping in your home, I always advise people to take care of it now before it becomes normalized. Once beeping in your home becomes normalized, you might put up with it for a few months or even a few weeks—and I've even seen people put up with it for a year. That's so incredibly unsafe because that beeping means something needs a replacement. The detector needs a new battery and it needs you to take care of it so it can protect you and take care of you in return.

ENTRANCES AND EXITS

When it comes to security, you think about the big things, like exits and entrances. However, many things can become an exit or entrance in your home, such as a window, so keep that in mind when you're considering how to keep people—and other creatures—out of your home.

There are several products I've recommended a great deal over the years that can help. One of them is a product called an Addalock. An Addalock is a small, inexpensive device you can put on the strike plate of your door and it can be installed in less than 30 seconds. You can even use this when you're on the go, such as staying in people's homes, hotels, or Airbnbs. It acts as a wedge between the door and the strike plate, preventing the door from being opened.

Patio doors are also points of weakness in a home. They usually don't have a very strong lock and are notoriously easy to break into. If a person has a simple tool or a picking tool, they can easily get in there and pull the lock up. So having something that could slide between the door and the outside trim can help keep you and everyone safe.

opens, it can grab the floor really firmly and can't be moved back. There are also door wedges with built-in alarms, such as the Door Stop Alarm from Sabre. This will make a very loud, shrill sound if the door is pressed against it, alerting you to the door being opened. Unfortunately, with enough pressure, the door can still be forced open, but this will buy you time and will help a great deal to keep you safe at a moment's notice.

And lastly, I highly recommend making sure that if you live in a home that's large or it's hard to hear the front door opening or the home has lots of windows, you get an inexpensive sensor alarm will be best for you. These door alarms are pretty simple and affordable. They come with two pieces that are installed with temporary mounting tape on the door or window and its frame. When the two pieces are separated by the opening of the door or window, an alarm will go off like a siren and alert you across the home, alert people nearby that there's an issue, and scare off any intruders. They can also be set to ding or announce every time the door or window is opened, so you can have protection and peace of mind when you're home. This tool can be invaluable and can go a long way toward keeping you safe.

Another option is a security bar. They're great, but they can be fairly expensive. If a security bar is outside your budget, you can get yourself a wooden broom, remove the broom head, and use the handle to install between the sliding door and its frame. This will block the door from opening from the outside even if it's unlocked.

As another added security for doors, I'd recommend a door wedge, which is a great little tool. You don't always need to install a chain, a double lock, or even a security lock for your rental because those can be damaging and are usually long-term solutions. A door wedge can actually do similar things without damaging anything. Getting yourself a really good rubber door wedge will go a long way—preferably the kind that has grips underneath so when the door

PETS AND CHILDREN

Another aspect of home safety and security to consider involves your little critters and your children. If you have small children or pets of any kind, it's imperative to remove their access to potentially harmful household items. When it comes to your critters and children, an ounce of prevention is worth a pound of cure. Getting a child safety kit, which comes with different types of locks for your home—toilet locks, cabinet locks, outlet covers, etc.—is a great place to start.

It's very easy to forget about how kids often view things with mystery and wonder, such as the toilet. I often call the toilet the "magic go-away hole." Many kids think a toilet is really fun to play with and that can cause so many problems, which is why using a lock can be so helpful. However, if they do get into the toilet and throw toys or other obstructions down there, the only way to fully extract an item is to completely remove the toilet from the base. Then you'd have to push the item from the bottom of the toilet out through the top and finally reinstall the toilet. We certainly don't want to have to do that!

Protecting the carpet and flooring is another crucial consideration in a rental home. I always tell people that rugs are a great way to protect the floors in your home. Inexpensive rugs, especially larger area rugs, can actually protect your carpet and floors in a pretty good way. They can prevent cat claw damage, spills and stains, and general wear and tear on your carpet, tile, or hardwood floors. Cats also love to beat up curtains and upholstered furniture. Investing in a few scratching posts and some cat tape to deter them from wreaking havoc in high-interest areas is a very smart move.

If you're having issues with stains on the carpet, a really good stain remover can do a good job. However, if a cat or dog urinates on the carpet, it can crystallize and leave a smell behind that can make it much more appealing for the cat or dog to do it in the same spot again and again. So make sure you neutralize that problem with vinegar and water. I've found over the years that more is better when it comes to vinegar on your carpet. Simply spray a vinegar and water mixture on the affected area, let it sit for 10–15 minutes, and then dab it dry with a clean cloth. Continue to repeat as necessary. The vinegar smell will dissipate pretty quickly, but if you're concerned about that, spread a little baking soda over it when it's dry and vacuum it up. This will help eliminate any remaining smells.

For hardwood floors, you can also use hydrogen peroxide to lighten dark stains from urine or water. Simply place a towel on the area, pour the hydrogen peroxide onto the towel until the towel is just damp, and let it sit for a few hours. Make sure to check on it regularly to see its progress. You can repeat this process a few times until the area is lightened enough that it's not as visible and then gently clean the area with water and your preferred floor cleaner. As always, make sure to test a small area before using this technique on larger areas.

Dogs love to beat up doors and trim, so it's important to get protective covers for your doors and your trims that are at dog level. There are plastic covers that install easily over your door handle or metal protective plates that can be secured with an adhesive.

When leaving your dogs at home alone, it's best to invest in a crate that's appropriate for their size. They also have crates that can be broken down and stored under a bed when you're home if space is limited. Leaving dogs in a room behind a closed door often can lead to destructive behavior and you might come home to a door or trim that's been completely destroyed. Providing a safe crate or another contained space can prevent damage to your home and prevent harm to your pups.

The truth is that things in the home can often get broken or beat up along the way and we don't know it's going to be a problem until it's too late. Rest assured that if you can catch it early, you're going to be okay. Letting problems go on longer can only compound the damage to the home you've created. Simply remind yourself that this is part of learning to care for your home and do your best to create safety and security for you and your loved ones.

TECHNICIANS IN YOUR HOME

I know what it's like to have a technician in your home and to feel like you need to hide parts of yourself. And that's okay. I sympathize and I understand. There have been many times where I've taken down my pride flags, hidden photos of myself and loved ones, and even concealed things that show I'm a trans person.

When you have a technician in your home, it's important to know that legally they need to treat you like a client and not someone they can take advantage of. In some states, it's okay to put a video camera up in your home to monitor your space when you're away. I always advise this, but know the laws when you do. You can find out more by googling your state and "security cameras in your apartment." You'll be able to find information specific to you. Even when it's legal, you'll still have to follow certain rules:

- Not facing cameras into other people's homes
- Keeping cameras out of private areas, like bathrooms
- Having your outdoor camera or doorbell camera visible and not hidden

You're also allowed to put signs up in your home indicating what rooms they're not allowed to go into and where the damage is. Any instructions you can lay out for your home are perfectly fine if you're not able to be home when a technician is there.

I always think it's best to remove any temptation by securing your valuables in your home. Money, jewelry, or anything valuable should be removed from visible sight. You'll want to also be mindful

that if you have a child, especially a toddler or someone under the age of 10, they should be taken outside the home for a little bit to make sure they're not around and interfering with the work. Many times, children have used my tools as toys or have grabbed my tools and run across apartments with them. That's incredibly dangerous! They're often really expensive tools. You don't want them to get damaged or lost in the process of your technician trying to help you.

Also be mindful if you have any pets or little critters that might be in the way. This is the time to put them in another room, crate them, or take them somewhere else to try to reduce any problems. Many times, dogs also treated my tools like they're something to play fetch with.

People are always asking me, "How can I be hospitable to the technician?" My answer is, it's not your job to be. You shouldn't have to be hospitable to be treated well. But if you want to care for them, then having water available is good and tea or coffee are nice, but they're not required either. Technicians will often ask to use your bathroom. I always think technicians shouldn't do this, but there are some occasions when you can't help that.

Be aware that things sometimes don't go as planned. A technician might think a job is going to take an hour, but then it ends up taking four hours. Sometimes, a four-hour job only takes 30 minutes. It's hard to know exactly how much time something's going to take because every apartment, plumbing, electrical problem, or drywall issue is a living, breathing situation. That being said, feel free to ask questions and get updates on the status of your project.

Most technicians love to talk about their work. They don't like to be undermined, but they do love to talk about what they know and their expertise. They want to know you appreciate them, and if they feel appreciated, they'll be happy to share how they did something and why they're doing something a certain way.

When someone is working in your home, there are other things you can do to make their work easier. Turn the air conditioner on, open a window, turn on a fan, or do anything you can to reduce the heat in your apartment when it's warm outside. Turn down the TV, video games, or music so sounds aren't too loud. And if you're working from home and you'll be in a meeting, you can call or email them to let them know or put a note on the door next to the handle so they know to be quiet. If there's anything else you need to tell the technician, make sure that if you're not able to communicate those things that you put it in visually on a note. Technicians will read it if it's by the door handle.

If there's anything you'd like the technician to know about entering your home, make sure to communicate that ahead of time. If you need them to knock, call ahead, or announce their arrival, put that information in the work request or put it in writing by emailing or texting them before they come to your apartment.

Regardless of whether you own or not, this is your home—and technicians should respect your space. If you set a boundary with a technician ahead of time and then they cross that boundary, then you have every right to stand up for yourself. It's your right as someone who's living there to feel safe in your space for however long your lease is. Be mindful that technicians are often underpaid and overworked. But that doesn't give them the right to treat you poorly or like you're part of the problem. You're simply asking them to do a service they're legally required to do.

Emotional Reset

It can be easy to overlook security and safety. Maybe you're living in a good part of a neighborhood and you think you're safe. But it's also important to know that everyone thinks they're safe until they're not, so taking precautions and thinking about these things ahead of time for protecting your loved ones, your home, and your belongings are vital. If you can put in a little effort, you can reduce the potential stress later. It's so overwhelming to deal with the fallout of a terrible situation or something gone wrong and it's so much better when you have a plan either written down or really thought out.

I'm so proud of you for thinking about this, even if it's stressful. You're doing a great job protecting yourself and everyone who lives in your home. Having peace of mind and feeling safe in your own home are human rights. You should feel safe in your home and you should be able to rest well at night—and I hope this information and encouragement help just a little.

MOVING OUT OF YOUR APARTMENT

PLANNING YOUR MOVE

When you're moving out of an apartment, it can be for a lot of different reasons: You're moving to a larger home, going on a new adventure, leaving a city, leaving a partner, moving out on your own, etc. One of the things you want to keep in mind is that moving out is taxing. I've moved to eight different apartments in the course of six years for various reasons—from breakups to sudden changes in work life. Sometimes, it was just for a change of space. I needed something different to feel safer or to feel better about my life. And knowing how to seek help for this is really important.

Two things I recommend when moving if you can afford one or both:

- Hiring movers to help for a couple hours
- Paying extra to move into the new place a month or week early so you have plenty of time to move

Of course, I'm not going to tell you to live outside your means and I'm not going to demand you get a mover, but I will say that an investment in a mover is really good and really important. It's a lot for one person to take on all by themselves and an hour or two of some paid hands can really take a lot of the burden off you.

If you have a hard time getting things from one place to another, there are local groups online, on Facebook, and on other social media sites that will help people move. Of course, be cautious and smart, and take the precautions that you need, but there are some good people out in the world who just want to help others. And I know they exist because I feel like I'm one of those people.

Understanding exactly when your lease is up is also so crucial for planning your move. I live in tropical Madison, Wisconsin, and because it's a college town, it's very common for lease start and end dates to not line up perfectly. If you find yourself in this situation, feel free to ask your landlord for an extension of a day or two.

Now be mindful—this might not actually work out. It's a game of luck and chance, but there's nothing wrong with asking so you can move right from one place to another with no gap. It's an honest question to ask and I'm proud of you for asking for things you need.

If you find yourself in need of a place to stay, it's okay to get a hotel for the night and it's okay to get a U-Haul for a night. It's okay to ask friends to let you crash with them. Anything you need to do to get by, that's okay. Sometimes, the best laid plans go awry!

The night before a move is always frantic—full of cleaning and repairs and general freak-outs. If you're able/can afford to get an overlap from one apartment to the next and move into the new place a week or a month or so before you move out, that's great. But that's a luxury a lot of people don't have—and that's okay. It's always been best for my mental health when I've had that luxury. When I didn't have a lot of money to spend, I'd spend it on that and move in a month early a little at a time rather than splurging for movers.

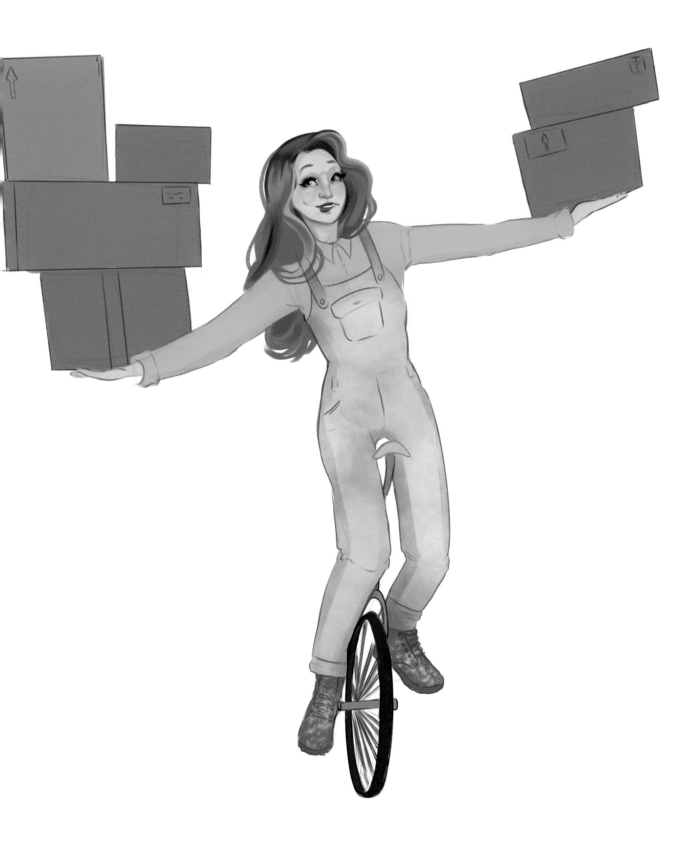

As you prepare to move, there are other things you should consider:

- Communicating boundaries with your landlord is important. Make sure you let them know when you're going to move out, ask how to return your keys, ask what needs to be done before you leave, complete your move-out checklist, etc.
- Have your mail forwarded to your new place. You can set it up ahead of time and have it scheduled to start on the day you move out/in.
- Switch your utilities over to your new place. If you have a gap in moving out/in dates, just let them know and they can usually separately schedule the end and start dates. This includes electricity, internet, water, etc.
- Plan to give yourself a minimum of one day with the empty apartment to clean and document everything.
- Turn in any keys, mail keys, fobs, etc., to the appropriate place you agreed to with your landlord.

If you forget something, hey, it's okay. Moving has so many moving parts (pun intended!) and I'll tell you, I've never moved well—I've always moved a little bit haphazardly. But hopefully these tips will help you feel a little bit more secure along the way.

GETTING YOUR DEPOSIT BACK

This is the biggest point of contention ever. Everybody asks me about getting the deposit back! I've laid out a lot of tips and tricks that might help you along the way to get it back—from wall repair to doors to windows to everything you can imagine. There are a lot of little things in this book that will set you up for success if you do them along the way. But I'm going to tell you a painful truth I've seen over the years—and that is you're probably not going to get it all back. A part of it—if not all of it—will probably be taken. They'll always find a way to reimburse their costs from the deposit. Yes, there are some legal things to be aware of, and Chapter 16, you'll get that information, but also be mindful about not expecting to get your deposit back.

If you get it back, yay. But the truth of the matter is, companies are really good at really pushing what the boundaries are when it comes to normal wear and tear because they shouldn't be taking a deposit from that. Now what does that mean? Normal wear and tear are things in the apartment that are going bad, like carpet being worn out, dings on the wall, a loose doorknob, etc. They're not supposed to charge you for that.

It's important to remember that everything I'm saying is also subject to someone else's opinion. We'd go into people's apartments very shortly after they moved out—like within an hour of people moving out—and we'd have to make decisions. It would sometimes be three to five of us going into these apartments together—it was an event for property managers. It was like their favorite part of the day was to find ways to charge people. It was like a game almost—and I hated being a part of it. It was awful. No matter what, I tried my best to make room for tenants to not be swindled.

But you know, I'd constantly be asked for specific things and it was always hard to give answers because I don't know—I haven't started the work yet—but they want to have that number right away to start working on charges. Like within the first couple hours, they were already trying to figure out how much to charge you. It's that type of game.

It's also important to remind people that property managers and maintenance technicians need to have an exact amount for what's going to be replaced. They can't give you a rounded-up estimate. They can't just say $50—they have to say $47.83. It has to be an exact amount. That's going to be important. Once they give you an itemized list, they better have the numbers attached to it or you could push back in a court of law to get your deposit back.

Cleaning is another big factor. If you have cats or dogs and they beat up the place or a room smells of cat urine, vinegar might not be enough. You might have to do a really deep clean and planning a few days ahead of time is going to ensure less of a headache when they do the full checkout. And if you're able to be there for the checkout, I highly recommend it. You can start pushing back right away. If you're not there for the checkout, that's okay, but just be mindful that there's no one there to push back on things on your behalf. And you could say it right away—you can call them out on it: "No, I asked nine times for this and here is all the emails and this was never repaired. I should'nt be charged for it because I've never had the full use of it." Those are important things to remember and you can always push back on the property manager and maintenance technician when you're there.

It's important to have an idea of what you might get charged for:

- **Painting:** Chances are you won't get charged for painting because it's something most landlords do anyway between tenants. Unless your walls are filthy or you painted them a different color paint when you moved in, you probably won't get charged for it.
- **Wall Damage:** Some are going to charge you $25 or so for a hole repair. It's not just how much each item costs—it's how many hours a technician spends on it. So if a technician gets paid $25 an hour and it takes an hour to repair something, they're going to charge you for that. And the repair time is much harder to push back on. The item itself is easier to push back on, but it's really hard to argue against the cost of labor. So use the tips in this book before moving out to save money on wall repairs.
- **Carpet:** Carpet is going to automatically be replaced after a certain amount of time—seven years is usually the standard—but that's not true everywhere. And in some states, there are actually laws about how often they have to replace the carpet. (See page 210.) If the carpet was brand new when you moved in and you're moving out within the first four years and there's significant damage to the carpet, they might charge you for that.
- **Appliances:** If there are any damaged appliances, you'll probably get charged unless there's documentation of it being damaged and you requested a repair. While they shouldn't charge you if they're planning to upgrade the appliance because of its age, they can still charge you if you broke the appliance and didn't give them the opportunity to repair it. They're much more

likely to replace the appliance because they're in a rush to get the apartment ready for the next tenant, but if you request a repair while you're there, they have the time and space to fix it for cheaper and hopefully not charge you for it.

- **Plumbing:** When it comes to plumbing issues, these are all things that will most likely be taken care of from the property management companies and not something you necessarily have to worry about. Keep in mind that if there's a significant leak or problems with a showerhead, parts are missing, etc., you might get charged. If you upgraded a showerhead, a sink, or any fixtures, keep the old ones and put them back before you leave. Property management companies will sometimes be pretty upset with fixtures being replaced and charge you for the repair, even though they'd do that anyways, or they're better off keeping the new stuff. It doesn't matter. They want all the things to look the same.

- **Pets:** There's a lot of debate about pet deposits and how they work. Pet deposits can be separate from other deposits—it all depends on what state you live in. It's often hard to distinguish between what was caused by a pet and what wasn't. They might even say the repair will cost more than the pet deposit was to begin with. A lot of times, they separate the pet deposit to make people feel secure, but in reality, it's just theatrics. It's not something that's ultimately going to protect you, so be prepared.

If you've lived in a place longer than six to seven years, I'd push back on a lot of stuff they might try to charge you for. Many of those things are just going to be normal repairs. There's going to be wear and tear on the doors, walls, garbage disposal, appliances—things are going to happen. That doesn't mean you're not going to not get charged, but keep all this in mind when you talk to your landlord about your deposit.

The more turnover the property management company has in the first year or two, the more expensive it could be because it can be more of a turnover every time. If it's one big turnover every 10 years, that's a lot cheaper than having to do a big overhaul every 6 months to a year. That's just a lot for these places to take on. Many places will do renovations and upgrades. If you know they're doing a renovation or upgrade in an apartment next to you before you move out, chances are they're going to upgrade your apartment anyways and you might not get charged for a lot of it. Sometimes, when they want to do a renovation, they might get a little bit loosey goosey with the idea of deposits and want to use some of the deposit to cover their costs of renovation. This isn't legal and they can't do this, so be mindful if that appears to be happening to you.

It's best to remember that most property management companies have high turnovers and the property managers when you move out might not be the same property managers from when you moved in. Even so, try your best to have the best relationship you can with the property manager—it's going to serve you better in the long run. And I know it can be difficult sometimes, but the property managers are the ones making the final call, not the company itself, and the company is going to rely on them.

Here's a checklist to consult before you move out:

- Locate the move-in checklist you filled out before you moved in. Most rentals require this and it highlights anything that was damaged before you moved in and is still damaged now.
- Take pictures and videos of everything in the apartment after you've cleaned and moved out to have proof of the state of the apartment when you left it. Get all the details up close.
- Make a list of all the requests you've put in for repairs that were never done and have the supporting texts and emails ready.
- Have a friend with you while you document everything—just to have another set of eyes in case it's ever your word against the landlord's.

This is often a stressful process—I hope not for you—but if it is, make time for yourself that day. Build in time to relax and breathe, have dinner with friends, hang out with a cat, etc. Do the things you need to do to make sure you're okay. It's stressful to communicate things to people who have more power than you and that's the case in these situations. No matter what the landlord, property manager, or technicians say, they're the ones holding more cards than you. And if you don't have a lot of room in your budget, it could be very stressful. So make time for yourself in any way you can. It might serve you well down the road. Being in the best mental space while you're doing this work is important for you and your decisions going forward.

Overall, it's very difficult to know for sure if you'll get your deposit back, but just be mindful to do the best you can, do the best cleaning you can, do the best repairs you can, but the longer you live at a place, the less likely you are to get the deposit back—and you're not alone. That happens.

PROTECTING YOUR VALUABLES AND HOME WHEN MOVING

When you're moving out of a place, it's important to keep all the things that are valuable to you. This is your TV, desks, bed frames, etc. So often when you're moving in and moving out, you cause damage. The majority of the damage happens when you're moving out.

Having ample time if possible, having a good plan, and having everything packed up when you move out are really important, but as someone who's also neurodivergent, I understand that packing ahead of time can be a luxury a lot of us don't have. And you can try your best, but you'll wait until the last minute—and that's just the truth of it sometimes.

A BRIEF CHECKLIST

- If you bought a new TV, computer, etc., always keep the box and the Styrofoam that comes with it. This is a great practice. Use your storage unit or an empty closet in your home to store these boxes. Keeping the boxes with the Styrofoam makes a world of difference when you're moving out and when you're doing big moves.

- You can also go to any hardware store and get yourself some type of foam or bubble wrap and then wrap it around the electronics. Start with cardboard, foam/bubble wrap, then cardboard again—and secure it all by wrapping tape around it several times. Make sure it's nice and tight and firm and that the tape is all the way around the packaging.

- Keep the corners of all the hallways and doors covered with cardboard to prevent damage when you're moving out.

- Keep everything in separate boxes that are going to be labeled "fragile" and indicate which side needs to be pointed up. All that will make a really big difference later on.

- You can use newspaper, paper towels, butcher paper, etc., to wrap your items. Wrap them individually and don't overpack breakables in your boxes.

- Pack breakable items with lots of towels or other light filler items so the box isn't too heavy and the breakables are cushioned.

- Never stack boxes labeled "fragile" or have other boxes stacked on top of them. If you're worried about certain items, get the rigid storage boxes to pack those breakables. They're often inexpensive and can be used even after you move.

- Use a dolly or a small folding hand truck. They can be found for about $50 and can save your breakables and your back. You can roll out two to three boxes at once. It can fold up

for easy storage and you'll find yourself using it all the time.

- Use towels and blankets for wrapping larger valuables—ones you're okay with getting a little dirty in the move.

- Get a large mattress bag for around $10 for a queen size. This will protect your mattress so it's not touching the floor when you move. It's essentially just a giant plastic bag.

- Try your best to label each of the boxes and totes you're using for moves to help you keep track of where everything is.

- Wrap your furniture with plastic wrap you get at a hardware store. Wrap each piece and all parts and corners several times with a nice thick layer. This will prevent scratching or other damages.

- Having sliders is also really important for moving. I highly recommend getting furniture sliders—they really make a huge difference. They usually have sticky tape that attaches to the feet or the corners of the bottom and the other side is smooth plastic. This will let you simply push the furniture around without damaging it or the floors. If you want, you can leave them on after the move for easy rearranging.

- Getting door wedges is super important so you can wedge open a door when you're moving things constantly.

- If you have a door that doesn't fit a wedge underneath, you can always put a flathead screwdriver on the ground and that will hold the door open.

- I use bungee cables a lot for holding doors open. If a door has some type of handle on it that you can wrap with a bungee cable and there's a railing on the side, you can always hold it open with the bungee cable instead of just putting a rock down on the floor.

- I'd err on the side of more trips than less trips. You're often trying to fit everything into one trip. It becomes a nightmare on its own if you try to throw everything in there. If you're able to do everything in one trip with one big truck, kudos to you. But if you're not, that's also okay. I've done upward of 15 trips if I've had to—and that's okay. Even as a professional, I know how hard it is sometimes—and I'm proud of you for doing what you can.

There will also be items you want to wait until the last minute to pack. I always like to make sure there's a large Tupperware, tote, or a bag that holds all my last minute-stuff. Sometimes, it's two or three totes.

As someone who's seen a lot of people move in and out, I'll tell you that the best moves were the ones who got the help they needed and did all the prep ahead of time. The hardest ones are when people feel like they're frantically moving. A lot of corners are going to be cut, but that's okay. I'm one who believes it is what it is sometimes—and I'm proud of you for doing what you can.

If you have to spend money later on to afford the loss of the deposit or pay extra because of the damages, hell, if it's worth it for you, I understand. I won't judge you and I support you. Landlords and property managers can think what they want, but you're more valuable than property and that's the most important thing you can take away from all this.

CLEANING

Part of getting your deposit back and leaving on good terms is to do a deep clean of the apartment after everything is moved out. That's why it's good to give yourself a few days in your old space by moving out before your deadline. If you can't and you're okay with losing the

deposit, that's also okay. Your landlord will pay someone to clean for them. The following tips will help you clean efficiently.

SURFACES

- One of the things that work best is having brush extensions for drills. If you have a stubborn shower that's just not getting cleaned, having brush extensions for a drill can be good. Make sure you don't crack the tiles with too much pressure. Go slow—don't overdo it. These also work well on toilets, sinks, floors, or anything else with a hard surface.

- Vinegar is such a helpful thing to have. I like to keep vinegar diluted with water in a spray bottle. Even when it comes to walls and floors, a little bit of water and just a tiny bit of vinegar can clean walls pretty effectively.

- Magic Eraser is great, but it's expensive. Get the off-brand kind called "melamine foam sponge." You get the same thing, but it's much, much cheaper. It's great for cleaning walls, getting scuff marks off tiles, and even polishing your appliances, like microwaves and ovens.

APPLIANCES

- Cleaning appliances is also important. Get the oven, dishwasher, and washer and dryer clean before you leave. You can use products made specifically for cleaning these or just do your best with what you have.

- Vinegar in a bowl heated in the microwave will help get muck and grime off easily.

- A top-load washer can handle vinegar being used in a washing cycle to clean, but it can damage rubber gaskets, so don't use it with your dryer or front-loader.

- Never use the self-cleaning option on an oven if it has it. That can actually cause more damage. Use a bit of baking soda to make a paste and use that to scrub. Wipe that off with vinegar and water.

CARPET

- There's always going to be a little bit of stuff that's on the carpet. Make sure to vacuum until there's barely anything getting into the vacuum bag or canister.
- Check with your landlord or property manager about their plans for the carpet. Sometimes, they'll be replacing it or shampooing it anyway.
- If they're not replacing it or having it professionally cleaned, you can rent a carpet cleaner—usually at your local hardware or grocery store—by the hour. I've done that before and to great success, especially for a trouble spot I knew was going to get me charged.

MISCELLANEOUS

- Let things soak with Goo Gone if there are sticky substances on a countertop. If there's sticky residue from command strips on the walls, using Goo Gone can also help with that.
- If you have a lot of oil-based things that are grimed up, dish soap does a really good job of cleaning. Just let it soak in a little bit.

You don't need to get super specific all the time. For example, cleaning the faucets and spouts on the tub. There is a good chance these types of things will get replaced anyways, and if not,

they'll get cleaned. The most important things are larger items, like appliances, the carpet, and any major repairs.

Keep in mind that the management company is going to be doing some cleaning after you move out anyways. Basic cleaning is something that's going to happen in every home. I've never seen a property management company not do cleaning in an apartment before a new tenant, but if you want to be that rare exception and do a deep clean and you have the time, go for it. But just know you might get charged for cleaning anyways because they might want to ensure it's extra clean after you move out.

Overall, you can ask your property managers what to look out for. If you ask the property manager, "Hey, what are things to look out for in my specific home?" they'll more than likely give you some ideas and tips. Some won't tell you a darn thing, but a lot of them will.

And if you ever have maintenance technicians in your home repairing something, just ask them: "Hey, what are some things you see? What are some issues I can take care of? What are things you'd be mindful of when you're moving out?" They'll give you some helpful hints that could help you down the road.

Emotional Reset

Moving out is one of the most stressful things anyone might ever do. Moving in can be stressful in a different way. It's full of new and unexpected things. But moving out—wow! I want you to take a moment right now and just breathe with me because moving out can bring up a lot of memories. It can bring up a lot of trauma, a lot of history, a lot of pain. Homes are so sacred, and when you move out, a lot of that can come back to you.

There have been times where moving out has felt like losing a friend. It's like all the memories of when I lost my mom come back to me. It's like the memories of when I got my divorce from my first marriage—they come back. You think about the things you went through in that home you inhabited. If you had a cat you lost and you're moving out, you might think about how there's fur there, there's smell there, there's so much of them in that space. And that's hard. I want you to take a moment here and remember that moving out is honoring those memories and honoring that lived-in experience you went through. You're not losing any of those things. You're just a person who has emotions and a life, and you lived a full and loving life in this space. And that's good.

The best landlords, the best people in this industry will want you to live a life there. And there's often this tug of war between tenants and property managers. The truth is that the best ones—the ones who get into the industry for good reasons—understand. And you understand how hard it can be sometimes as a tenant yourself. And I just want you to know I'm proud of you for doing what you need to do. I'm proud of you for reading this chapter. I'm proud of you for living a life that's full of new things. You're a wonderful human who deserves the best. And I hope you're leaving here to go somewhere else where you're equally as loved as you have been in your life and that this is a positive change.

If you feel like you're losing something, just know you're not alone. That happens to all of us at moments in our life. And this isn't a failure. This is just a moment in your life that will pass. So please think ahead, take the moments you need, and practice self-care in any way you can to make sure you're safe. Reach out to friends to make sure you're taken care of. And above all else, remember you're human and that changes are human. I love you.

PART 3

★

RESOURCES

TENANT LAWS AND RESOURCES FOR EVERY STATE

KNOWLEDGE IS POWER

Renter's rights can vary from state to state, city to city, and even within counties. There are many different laws across the United States, so it's important to know the laws in your area so you can protect yourself and your home from landlords who don't have your best interests at heart.

The most renter-friendly states are Vermont, Delaware, Oregon, Rhode Island, and Nevada. Some of the states with the least amount of renter protections are Arkansas, West Virginia, Louisiana, Georgia, and Wyoming.

Some states that have exceptional rights for renters offer the following protections:

- Security deposit limits
- Repair policies that allow you to deduct costs from your rental payments for repairs you have to make
- Requirements for landlords to provide notice before entering your home
- Restrictions on rent increases
- Renter-friendly rules regarding eviction from a premises

While there are many differences, many states also have similar protections for all renters. All states but Arkansas recognize the implied right of habitability of a rental, although many cities or counties in Arkansas do have laws regarding a livable dwelling.

According to NOLO.com, in most places, landlords are responsible for:

- Keeping basic structural elements of the building safe, including floors, stairs, walls, and roofs
- Maintaining all common areas, such as hallways and stairways, in a safe and clean condition
- Keeping electrical, plumbing, sanitary, heating, ventilating, and air-conditioning systems and elevators operating safely
- Supplying cold and hot water as well as heat in reasonable amounts at reasonable times
- Keeping known environmental hazards, such as lead paint, dust, and asbestos, from posing a significant danger
- Taking reasonable measures to prevent foreseeable criminal intrusions
- Exterminating rodents and other vermin

No disclaimer can waive these rights, even if it's written into a lease or another legal document.

FEDERAL LAWS

Several federal laws can protect you as a renter. Knowing your rights can help you secure housing if you think someone's trying to prevent you from renting.

THE FAIR HOUSING ACT

The Fair Housing Act protects all renters across the United States. It prohibits discrimination in housing because of:

- Race
- Color
- National origin
- Religion

- Sex (including gender identity and sexual orientation)
- Familial status
- Disability

The law also makes it illegal to harass you because of all these same factors.

For people with disabilities, housing providers must make reasonable accommodations and allow reasonable modifications that might be necessary to allow persons with disabilities to enjoy their housing.

Under this law, landlords also can't limit the number of children in a unit, restrict their use of common areas, or require families with children to live on certain floors or in certain units. The only exception to this is "housing for older persons" or grown children who are legal adults.

Another form of discrimination that this law prevents is discrimination in housing advertisements. These ads might say or imply that certain people aren't welcome or that there's a preference for a certain type of applicant.

If you ever find yourself in a situation where you feel like your rights are being violated, you can file a complaint with the Office of Fair Housing and Equal Opportunity at www.hud.gov/fairhousing/fileacomplaint.

FAIR CREDIT REPORTING ACT

Passed in 1970, the Fair Credit Reporting Act prevents landlords from being able to run your credit without permission. It also requires a landlord to notify you if your credit report is the reason why they're denying your application.

AMERICANS WITH DISABILITIES ACT

Under the ADA, landlords are required to allow service animals. Service animals must be licensed, registered, and vaccinated according to local laws. Please note, though, that there's no federal registration requirement and your local laws might not require the licensing or registration of service animals. Please read more about the animal laws in your area.

LGBTQIA+ TENANTS RIGHTS

The HUD Equal Access rule requires equal access to Housing and Urban Development programs. This includes properties that receive HUD funding or loans for LGBTQIA+-identifying people, regardless of sexual orientation, gender identity, or marital status.

There have also been a couple new rulings and orders that further protect the LGBTQIA+ community. In 2020, in the case of *Bostock v. Clayton County* (Georgia), the Supreme Court explicitly looked at sex discrimination laws, civil rights, and protected classes on the basis of sexual orientation and gender identity. The court decided that Title VII of the Civil Rights Act, which forbids discrimination in the workplace on the basis of sex, would also forbid discrimination because of sexual orientation or gender identity.

In 2021, the Biden Administration issued Executive Order No. 13,988, which stated: "Under Bostock's reasoning, laws that prohibit sex discrimination ... also prohibit discrimination on the basis of gender identity or sexual orientation, so long as the laws do not contain sufficient indications to the contrary." This included the Fair Housing Act, Title IX, the ACA, and the Equal Credit Opportunity Act (ECOA). This executive order protects the LGBTQIA+ community from a variety of discriminatory practices.

LEGAL RESOURCES

Being a renter and not knowing your rights can be scary, but the fact that you've read this far means you're doing everything you can and I'm so proud of you. You also need to know that it's okay to ask for help and you shouldn't have to go through this alone. There are so many resources available, and while they're great resources, they do often make it hard for those of us who have learning disabilities, struggle with tasks, or have mental health issues, such as anxiety. That being said, many people at these organizations do want to help you! Please reach out today and ask for assistance if you need it or keep these resources handy if you should ever need them in the future.

Organizations such as nonprofit legal aid providers can often be found in your area that offer free or low-cost legal help. You can also reach out to your local state's bar association for help finding an affordable lawyer in your area. LawHelp.org is also a great resource. Use the QR code on this page to locate more links and information for legal help in your area.

Emotional Reset

All this information I've laid out for you can be very overwhelming. You might feel like you're drowning in a sea of information and it can be isolating when it feels like no one's on your side. But hopefully, with the information in this chapter, you can feel more seen and supported. In circumstances that require us to reach out for help as renters, we might often not get the desired outcome we seek. The system can be against us, but it doesn't mean you shouldn't try. I'm proud of you for taking matters into your own hands and seeking help to find justice. Remember to take a deep breath, do what you can when you can, and know that you're not alone. Often, that's all we need to remind us of our own humanity.

INDEX

A

accordion plunger, 68
Addalock, 187
adhesive, repairing/replacing vinyl
    baseboards with, 143
adjustable pliers, 56, 57, 58, 75, 76,
    92, 93
advertisements, housing, 211
aerator, faucet. See faucet aerator
air carriage plungers, 66
air conditioners/air conditioning,
    178–180
    cleaning, 179
    intake/return filters, 178
    lack of, as emergency request, 44
    protecting during the winter, 165
    window units, 179–180
alarms, security, 188
Allen keys, 56, 58, 77, 175
aluminum racks, 30
amenities, apartment, 22
Americans with Disabilities Act (ADA),
    211
anchors, drywall, 120–122. See drywall
    anchors
ant baits, 166
anti-stick scissors, 143
ants, 166
apartment
    construction-grade materials in
        your, 30–31
    creating a home in your, 31–33
    documenting everything when
        moving into, 34
    as a home rather than someone
        else's property, 36–37
    moving out of, 194–205
    moving out of your, 194–203
    thoroughness for reviewing
        checklist when moving into,
        28–29
apartment, looking for an, 16–25
emotions and difficulties with, 17
    financing, 18
    reading/signing a lease, 23–24
    safety and, 19–20
    touring an apartment when, 20–22
appliances, 170–182
air conditioners, 178–180
    cleaning, when moving out,
        202–203
    dishwashers, 176–177
    garbage disposals, 174–175

getting charged for damaged,
    197–198
instruction manuals for, 181
ovens, 173–174
refrigerators/freezers, 170–172
washing machines, 180–181
Arkansas, 210
asbestos, 210
auger. See drain auger/snake

B

baking soda
    cleaning oven with, 203
    for eliminating vinegar smells with,
        189
    used for smelly drains, 78
baseboards, repairing and replacing,
    143
basin wrench, 72
bathrooms. See also faucets; sinks;
    toilets
    caulking in, 81–83
    faucet repairs in, 72–73
    fixing a loose shower handle in,
        d101
    fixing a whistling shower faucet or
        tub diverter in, 102
    fixing a whistling showerhead in,
        101
    low water pressure in sinks, 74–77
    maintenance technicians using
        your, 190
    mold in, 162, 163
    removing/repairing tub plugs in,
        80
    replacing a showerhead in, 100
    replacing/repairing sink stoppers
        in, 79
    showers, 100–102
    smelly drains in, 78
    unclogging sink drain in a, 66–71
bathtubs, removing and repairing
    plugs of, 80
bedbugs, 166
beehive plunger, 88
bellows plungers, 88
Biden Administration, 211
bidets, 93–94
bifold doors, fixing, 139
Bio-Clean, 71
black mold, 162, 167
blackout curtains, 166

bleach
    cleaning a toilet auger with, 89
    for cleaning plungers, 88
    mold and, 162
blinds
    repairing, 123
    replacing mini, 125
    replacing slats on, 124
Bondo putty, 141
Bostock v. Clayton County (2020), 211
box cutters, 57
box fans, 166
break-ins, as an emergency request,
    44
breaker boxes
    labeling, 150
    outlet replacement and, 152
    testing, 150–151
breathe, as step in troubleshooting
    process, 52
brushes, paint, 60, 114, 116, 117
builder-grade materials and
    equipment, 30, 31, 35
building inspector, 44
bungee cables, 201
burns, 34

C

cabinets
    checking when you first move into
        your apartment, 28
    fixing an improperly hung door on,
        140
    loose/stripped screw holes and,
        130–131
calcium buildup, around sink faucet,
    72
California patch method, 109, 110–111
cameras, security, 19, 190
carbon monoxide detectors, 33, 186
carpeting
    checking when you first move into
        your apartment, 28
    cleaning, when moving out, 203
    getting charged for, when moving
        out, 197
    lease terms and, 24
    looking for an apartment and wear
        and tear of, 20, 21
    repairing corrugated, 142
    stains on, 189
catwalks, 19

V

ACKNOWLEDGMENTS

To my best friend, my biggest support, and my hero, my spouse mouse Ari Gochberg. You taught me that no tools in life were as important as the ones that it took to love myself.

Also to Maggie Conrad, my business partner and my sister. You make my dreams a reality with your tenacity and compassion.

And lastly to my Mom. You may not be here to read this but I know that you would be proud of the daughter that you brought into this world.

MERCURY STARDUST (@mercurystardust), the Trans Handy Ma'am, is a professional home maintenance technician and award-winning activist. Mercury credits her TikTok success to her experience teaching burlesque, where she learned to communicate and create a safe space for students who had frequently experienced trauma. She's been featured in stories by NBC, NPR, Buzzfeed, *Newsweek, The Washington Post,* and Pink News. Her leadership within the trans community has led to collaborations with such brands as Dolby, Lowe's, and Point of Pride.